W9-BXX-891

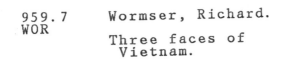

GEORGE ROGERS CLARK
LIBRARY MEDIA CENTER

959.7   Wormser, Richard.
WOR
               Three faces of
                 Vietnam.

                                    11BT00784

$20.50

DATE			
NOV 20 2005			

G R CLARK JR SR HG
1921 DAVIS AVE
WHITING, IN 46394

GEORGE ROGERS CLARK
LIBRARY MEDIA CENTER
BAKER & TAYLOR

THREE FACES OF
VIETNAM

THREE FACES
OF
VIETNAM

RICHARD L. WORMSER

FRANKLIN WATTS
NEW YORK CHICAGO LONDON TORONTO SYDNEY

Photographs copyright © : Wide World Photos:
pp. 15, 126, 143;
All other photographs copyright © The National Archives.

Library of Congress Cataloging-in-Publication Data

Wormser, Richard, 1933–
Three faces of Vietnam / Richard L. Wormser.
p.   cm.
Includes bibliographical references and index.
Summary: Examines the Vietnam War from the perspectives of antiwar
protesters, the Vietnamese people, and the American soldiers who
fought in the war.
ISBN 0 531 11142-3
1. Vietnamese Conflict, 1961–1975—Juvenile literature.
[1. Vietnamese Conflict, 1961–1975.]   I. Title.
DS557.W68   1993
959.704'3—dc20   93-11099 CIP AC

Copyright © 1993 by Richard L. Wormser
All rights reserved
Printed in the United States of America
6 5 4 3 2

CONTENTS

To Elaine, for her kindness

1
PRELUDE TO A REBELLION

It was called the "Nifty Fifties," the "Good Old Days," the "Fabulous Fifties."

The 1950s was an era of the Hula-Hoop and 3-D movies, tail-finned Cadillacs and haircuts that looked like a duck's rear end, Patti Page and Pat Boone, the convertible and the "passion pit"—the name teenagers gave to the drive-in movie. It was an era in which success in life was determined by what you owned and how much money you earned. For most middle-class white teenagers, life was orderly and dull. Tom Hayden, who would become one of the leaders of the antiwar movement in the 1960s, remembered growing up in suburban Detroit in the 1950s.

> For most young people like myself, the world was largely a one-dimensional one. . . . There seemed to be only one reality, one set of values, those of the comfortable middle class. . . . life was already programmed. You went to high school, then college, you got married or found a job.[1]

The material values of the generation that grew up in the 1950s was a reflection of their parents' achievements.

Many adults of that generation had lived through the Great Depression and the Second World War, both of which shaped their thinking. Their goal was to make life better for their children than it was for them. Parents who had gone as far as high school wanted their kids to go to college. If the parents worked in a factory, they wanted their children to work in offices or become professionals. They made sacrifices so that their children could reap the benefits. Tom Hayden's description of his parents could fit millions of American families in the 1950s.

> Loyal and patriotic Americans, they lived in a world of big families, small communities and a permanent circle of friends. They sought no greener grass nor new frontiers . . . they were already home. They took the American dream as their goal and their working lifetimes as a means to achieve it. . . . By nature they were populists who resented any elites who took advantage of ordinary people, but their feelings were expressed in no public form. . . . The values they did impart were those they tried to live by: education, enterprise, fairness.[2]

For many young people growing up in the rural parts of America, life was particularly uncomplicated. James Seddon, who would eventually fight in Vietnam, remembered his childhood with a great deal of pleasure.

> Like many Iowa boys, my days were filled with swimming in the pond and hoeing in the garden, milking cows and eating corn on the cob. We built cabins and dug holes. At night, we slept under the big maple tree in the front yard. We played hide-and-seek and told ghost stories. If we were feeling especially brave, the graveyard down the road pro-vided enough good, healthy terror to keep us awake all night. My life was not only filled, it was fulfill-

ing. . . . Each day brought new, exciting and undiscovered places. . . . The school was the center of the community and everyone gathered there for some activity sooner or later. . . . It was not just a place of learning, but a place where people cared.[3]

Like many young people, Seddon accepted without question a value system that had its origins in the nineteenth century, when the country was still young and had complete faith in itself:

I had been raised to follow the rules, to be a good citizen and obey the laws of my country and follow the morals of society. I always thought the laws and morals applied to everyone in the same way and were for the good of everyone; that they were the way people aspired to the loftier ideals of mankind, with the hope of improving the lives of all. . . .[4]

But despite the survival of traditional values and the economic prosperity of the country, there was much anxiety in America. The Cold War between the United States and the Soviet Union cast its shadow over the nation. In 1950, Senator Joseph McCarthy of Wisconsin started a hysterical anticommunism crusade that would maintain an atmosphere of fear over American life throughout most of the decade. McCarthy engineered and manipulated a panic by accusing people of being communists or "soft on communism" without any evidence to back up his assertions. However, to many, his charges seemed plausible, especially when spy rings were uncovered and two Americans, Julius and Ethel Rosenberg, were arrested, tried, convicted, and executed for allegedly passing atomic secrets to the Soviet Union. Their death sentence caused mass protests throughout the country and the world. In 1951 fuel was added to the fires of anticommunism when communist North Korea attacked

Senator Joseph McCarthy initiated an
anticommunism campaign that falsely accused
thousands of Americans of being either
communists or communist sympathizers.

the Republic of South Korea, and the United States and its allies went to war to defeat "communist aggression." There was a growing fear of atomic war throughout the country. Families built or installed bomb shelters in their backyards and stocked them with several months' supply of food and water. Schoolchildren practiced bomb drills and were instructed in how to protect themselves by hiding under their desks.

All of these events led America to turn on itself. Anybody who dissented from the mainstream of thought was branded a "communist" and could lose his job or be ostracized by friends, neighbors, and even relatives. There was tremendous pressure to conform to accepted community values. Dissenters and protesters were regarded with deep suspicion. Anyone who advocated "mixing of the races" or "free love" or "free thought" was branded a radical or communist and subjected to harassment, ostracism, dismissal from a job, and even jail. Ron Kovic, who would serve as a soldier in Vietnam, remembered his obsession with communism as a child:

> The Communists were all over the place back then. And if they weren't trying to beat us in outer space, . . . I [was] certain they were infiltrating our schools and trying to take over our classes and control our minds. We were certain that one of our teachers was a Communist . . . and we promised to report anything new he said in our history class that year.[5]

Teenagers were urged to be clean, wholesome, religious, asexual, to abstain from alcohol (drugs had not even entered the consciousness of most Americans), to be patriotic and good.

The values of America were often expressed in popular music of the day. Pop music was family music. Parents and their children listened to romantic ballads and novelty songs. For most of white America, popular music was wholesome, highly romantic, sentimental, shallow, and innocuous, avoiding sex beyond kissing and reinforcing traditional values about marriage, family, and God.

In 1951 a chance event happened that would mark the beginning of a change in youth attitudes. A disc jockey in Cleveland, Ohio, by the name of Alan Freed walked into a downtown music store and saw a group of white kids dancing to black music. It was called R & B, rhythm and blues, although many white racists contemptuously referred to it as "race music." The term reflected the racial attitudes that many white Americans held about blacks. R & B music was considered obscene by most white parents and they did not want their children contaminated by it. It was too raw, sexy, filled with emotion, and had a beat.

Alan Freed broke down this barrier when he decided to air R & B on his program. He changed the name from "rhythm and blues" to "rock and roll," and a new era was born. Despite parental protests and outrage, rock and roll took off. A generation gap had appeared, and the rift was beginning to widen.

The turning point came in Memphis, Tennessee, when a young Memphis truck driver walked into a studio to record a song and made music history. His name was Elvis Presley. To millions of adults, Elvis was their worst nightmare. He flaunted his sexuality in both his lyrics and movements. His music had a beat, feeling, and passion. Teenagers went wild over him—to the anguish of their parents. Elvis was a musical force of nature who overwhelmed his opposition and opened the floodgates. Rock and roll became a form of music that appealed to all teenagers. It provided a bond that linked rich and poor, white and black, in terms of their one common denominator—youth. Rock and roll contributed to subverting the ideals of conformity and niceness that parents had tried hard to impose upon their teenage children. Jerry

A new era was born with the birth of rock and roll.
A young southerner, Elvis Presley, made music
history by giving America's teenagers their own
music. Rock and roll helped to widen the generation
gap between young listeners and their elders.

Rubin, who was to become one of the leaders of the antiwar movement, wrote:

> *Elvis Presley . . . [turned] our uptight young bodies*
> *around. Hard animal energy beat/surged hot*
> *through us/the driving rhythm aroused repressed*
> *passions.*
> *Music to free the spirit.*
> *Music to bring us together.*[6]

Music was not the only sign of a growing split between teenagers and their parents. The 1950s witnessed the rise of the loner, the rebel, and the juvenile delinquent, who became cult figures in books and movies. Marlon Brando electrified teenage audiences in the movie *The Wild One,* when he played the role of a tough, yet sensitive head of a motorcycle gang that terrorizes a town. When a young woman in the film challenges him by asking, "What are you rebelling against?", Brando snarls in reply, "What have you got?"

The following year another lonely, rebellious figure became a teenage hero. James Dean starred in a film called *Rebel Without a Cause.* However, Dean's character in the movie, Jim Stark—unlike Brando's working-class character—represents a middle-class rebel. Stark, symbolizing the growing alienation of middle-class youths from their parents, chooses delinquency because he sees it as the only way to save himself from a meaningless adult society.

Another fictional character that caught the growing restive mood of many middle-class young people in the 1950s was that of Holden Caufield, the anguished teenage antihero of J. D. Salinger's novel *Catcher in the Rye.* Caufield narrates his life story from a mental institution in which he has been confined since his breakdown. Caufield is a searcher for purity in a world in which everyone is phony and corrupt. He envisions himself doing noble acts in an ignoble world, and the conflict creates the mental breakdown. Having been kicked out of prep school for the fourth time, he is unwilling to tell his parents what has happened. Instead, he wanders around the streets of New York, reflecting on his life and the inability of adults to notice what is really going on. In a moment of anguish, he describes to his would-be girlfriend the hypocrisy he found in his former school:

> It's full of phonies and all you do is study so you can be smart enough to be able to buy a goddamn Cadillac someday, and you have to make believe you give a damn if the football team loses, and all you talk about is girls and liquor and sex all day, and everybody sticks together in these dirty, goddamn little cliques.[7]

Comfortable middle-class morality was given an other jolt when a group of bearded, scruffy-looking literary bohemians burst upon the American scene and sent tremors down the spine of conservative Americans. They were called the Beat Generation—beat referring to the beat of music, although most Americans thought it referred to their physical appearance. Their life-style and their literature were the opposite of everything most people in America believed in. They were against materialism, consumerism, conformity, patriotism, and anti-communism. They were for free and open sexual relations, experimentation with drugs, communal living, integration, jazz—everything that most Americans opposed. Allen Ginsberg, the most celebrated poet of the group, savagely condemned America for what it was doing to its people in his poem "Howl":

> I saw the best minds of my generation destroyed by madness,
> Staring hysterical naked

*Dragging themselves through the Negro streets at dawn
    looking for
An angry fix.*[8]

"Howl" was followed by another literary hand grenade that exploded in the youth culture, Jack Kerouac's novel *On the Road.* Its main character, Dean Moriarity, explores the subterranean life of America as he and his friends and companions hitchhike back and forth across the country. The heroes of the book were a new breed of explorers and adventurers. Instead of seeking new continents or oceans, they "prowled in the wilderness," seeking out the forgotten, the unforgiven, the pariahs of America, whom they saw as wise men. The "beatniks," or "beats," hitchhiked or drove throughout America seeking mystical experiences in sex, drugs, jazz, and each other. "I could hear a new call and see a new horizon and believe it at my young age," wrote Kerouac. ". . . Somewhere along the line I knew there'd be girls, visions, everything; somewhere along the line I knew the pearl would be handed to me."[9]

The beatniks lived hand-to-mouth in a life-style that was a direct denial of the materialistic American way of life. Kerouac dismissed the educational institutions that prepared young people for a life in the system as:

> *. . . nothing but grooming schools for the middle class non-entity which usually finds perfect expression in . . . rows of well-to-do houses with lawns and television sets in each living room with everybody looking to the same thing and thinking the same thing.*[10]

The beats were satirized, castigated, criticized, chastised, investigated, threatened, feared, and hated by the "respectable people." Their numbers were small (there were a lot of people who played at being beat on the weekend), but their impact on the consciousness of young people was great. It helped shape the thinking of many like Tom Hayden:

> *In the coming years, I too hitchhiked to every corner of America, sleeping in fields here, doorways there, cheap hotels everywhere, embracing a spirit of the open road without knowing where I wanted to go. . . . The "new frontier" was on the road, not in the suburban life that tamed the human spirit. The personal instinct to take risks and journey into an emotional and intellectual universe had to be expressed.* [11]

By the end of the 1950s, great social forces began to stir deep within America like sleeping giants about to waken. In 1957, in Birmingham, Alabama, a young black minister by the name of Martin Luther King, Jr., led a bus strike that resulted in integrated buses, the first form of integration in the Deep South in over one hundred years. In 1958, 10,000 black and white students marched in Washington, D.C., demanding that schools be integrated. Tom Hayden sensed the discontent with the status quo:

> *It was the boring and prearranged nature of this existence that carried the first faint irritations that would grow into rebellion later. Among my circle of friends, there was little excitement or challenge in the life given us, nothing much to dream about or look forward to. As we grew in creativity and independence, we felt stifled by parents, school and church. We sneered at "brownnosers," those students who would do anything to please teachers. It seemed as if everything important had to be discussed in our cars or [at] pizza parlors, not in the proper institutions. You couldn't discuss sex with your parents, you couldn't discuss whether God*

existed with the nuns, you couldn't discuss how boring school was with your teachers. Instead, we had to memorize the answers to everything whether we agreed or not, and found we could be rewarded and advanced only in this way. [12]

Yet, it would be misleading to say that all young people were ready to rebel. Most American youth accepted without question the conservative values of their parents. But for those who felt a discontent and whose psychological receivers were tuned in to the airwaves of underground America, they were able to pick up these subterranean rumblings. Kenneth Rexroth, a poet and prose writer, warned parents what was starting to happen:

Listen—do you really think your kids are like bobby-soxers in those wholesome Coca-Cola ads? Don't you know that across the table from you at dinner sits somebody who looks at you as an enemy who is planning to kill him in the immediate future? Don't you know that if you were to say to your English class, "It is raining," they would take it for granted you were a liar? Don't you know they can never tell you nothing . . . that they simply can't get through, can't and won't even try to communicate? Don't you know this really? If you don't, you're headed for a terrible awakening. [13]

PRELUDE TO A
SECOND WAR

I n 1954, the same year that Elvis Presley walked into
Sun Studio in Memphis and changed American music
and the beatniks were scandalizing America, major events
were taking place in a country in Southeast Asia that few
Americans even heard of. In Geneva, Switzerland, dip-
lomats from France, China, England, and the Soviet
Union negotiated an end to a seven-year bloody war
between France and Vietnam. The United States did not
participate in the negotiations, attending merely as an
observer.

The war between France and Vietnam officially began after the end of World War II. But in reality it had
been going on for over a hundred years, ever since the
French occupied Vietnam in the nineteenth century. They
had been driven out by the Japanese in the Second
World War, but had returned after Japan's defeat. The
Vietnamese, who fiercely desired independence, resisted,
and war broke out.

The struggle for freedom was nothing new to the
Vietnamese people. From 300 years before Christ to
1,500 years after, they continuously battled the Chinese.
The Chinese won more battles and dominated Vietnam-

ese political and social life, but the Vietnamese never gave up their dream for freedom. In the end, their desire proved stronger than their enemy's greater size and strength. In 1462 the emperor Le Loi decisively defeated the Chinese at the battle of Tot Dong, and Vietnam was free.

Freedom was relatively short-lived. In 1535, Antô-nio Da Faria, a Portuguese merchant seaman, arrived in Vietnam to establish trade between Portugal and the Orient. The venture was not successful. But where traders failed, missionaries succeeded. In the seventeenth century, French Catholic priests were welcomed reluctantly by the emperors of Vietnam. The Vietnamese, while suspicious of the priests' religion and their political motives, wanted the scientific and military knowledge of the West. Catholicism opened the door to European influence, and the French rushed in to dominate Vietnam.

The French priests were extremely successful in converting the people. Hundreds of thousands of Vietnamese accepted Catholicism for political and economic reasons as well as religious ones. Merchants found that being Catholic was good for business with the French. Farmers used Catholicism to escape from the harsh political rule of the Vietnamese mandarins (public officials), who had adopted Chinese Confucianism as their religion because it stressed loyalty and obedience to the state.

In 1847, Vietnamese opposition to French rule began. France used this resistance as an excuse to send troops into the country. It was an era of colonialism, when all the major European powers were competing to establish colonies in Asia and Africa, usually by military force. In 1861 the Vietnamese emperor Tu Duc appealed in vain to Abraham Lincoln for American support. He was not the last Vietnamese leader who would ask America for help against the French. Almost one hundred years later, Ho Chi Minh was to make the same request and was also turned down—with tragic consequences for America and Vietnam.

22

By 1887 the French had conquered the countryside despite fierce Vietnamese resistance. They were brutal invaders, burning homes, looting villages, killing men, and raping women wherever they went. They burned one of the great Vietnamese libraries, destroying hundreds of thousands of manuscripts. The French then proceeded to divide the country into three parts—Cochinchina, Annam, Tonkin—which, collectively, along with Cambodia, they called Indochina.

The Vietnamese continued to fiercely resist the French. In 1859 they began a guerrilla movement in the swampy areas outside the city of Saigon that would last for almost a hundred years. They used hit-and-run tactics to attack French troops and then disappeared into the swamps and jungle. In 1862, Admiral Bonnard, the French commander, issued a report that would sound disturbingly familiar 100 years later:

> We have enormous difficulty in enforcing our authority. . . . Rebel bands disturb the country everywhere. They appear from nowhere in large numbers, destroying everything, and disappear into nowhere.[1]

Capitalists followed on the heels of the French army. Their goal was to become rich at any cost, the cost usually paid by the Vietnamese people. Paul Doumer, the governor-general of Indochina, developed the opium trade, thus establishing a deadly business in narcotics that would eventually lead to the addiction of millions of people. Doumer also reversed the rice policy of the Vietnamese emperors, who had forbidden farmers to export rice in order to ensure there was enough food for their own people. The French exported rice, making Vietnam one of the world's biggest suppliers of the grain. This policy not only created famine among the poor, but caused thousands of farmers to lose their lands to both the French and rich Vietnamese speculators.

The French also ruthlessly developed Vietnam's rubber industry. French industrialists, supported by the French government, used Vietnamese forced laborers to work their plantations. One of these recruiters, André Bazin, who recruited workers by kidnapping them, was murdered by the Vietnamese, but the practice continued. Workers died by the thousands of malaria, dysentery, and malnutrition. On one plantation alone, 12,000 out of 45,000 workers died between 1917 and 1944.

In 1911, at the height of France's economic and political oppression of Vietnam, a nineteen-year-old Vietnamese youth boarded a freighter bound for France. His name was Nguyen Sinh Cong. During his lifetime, he would be known by many different names, the most famous of which was Ho Chi Minh, which in Vietnamese means "Bringer of Light."

Ho fell in love with Paris and French culture and learned to speak French fluently. But he remained a dedicated Vietnamese patriot determined to see his nation free from French rule. In 1919, when President Woodrow Wilson traveled to Versailles to determine the peace after the end of World War I, Ho appealed to him to support Vietnam's desire for constitutional reforms and democratic freedom. Wilson did not reply.

In 1920, as the Russian Revolution of 1916 captured the imagination and support of people throughout Europe, Ho turned to communism as the means to free his country. Ho became a revolutionary, although he was basically interested in freeing his own country rather than in promoting revolution throughout the world. The Soviet Union offered to help him, and in 1924, Ho went there to study revolutionary tactics. Soon he was preparing Vietnamese students for the day when they would rise up to free their country.

In the late 1920s and early 1930s, Vietnam was shaken by a series of disorders and riots. Nationalist groups tried to incite uprisings which, after some initial successes, were crushed with the severest brutality.

French airplanes began to bomb villages suspected of hiding and sheltering insurgents. To add to the country's problems, the Great Depression of 1929 caused many industries to collapse, creating mass unemployment and labor unrest. Ho Chi Minh responded to the disorder by officially organizing the Indochinese Communist Party. The historic event took place at a British soccer match in Hong Kong which Ho used as a cover for his meeting with other communist leaders. His program was simple—an independent Vietnam and a worker-farmer government.

In 1939, Hitler invaded Poland and plunged the world into war. The Japanese, who had already invaded China and Mongolia, turned their armies loose on the colonial empires of Britain and France in Southeast Asia. Unlike other Vietnamese, Ho did not see Japan's victory as a step toward Vietnamese independence. He was more fearful of the Japanese than he was of the French. He supported the Allies who were fighting the Japanese, especially the United States. He believed that they would eventually win the war and hoped that, in return for his cooperation, they would support his claim for Vietnam's freedom.

In 1941, after a thirty-year exile, Ho Chi Minh returned to his country disguised as a Chinese journalist. There he met with two men who were to play instrumental roles in their country's future: Pham Van Dong, who would become prime minister, and Nguyen Giap, who would command the Vietnamese armies. Ho felt it was time to organize "patriots of all types and ages, peasants, workers, merchants and soldiers." This new organization was called the Vietnam Independence League—the Viet Nam Doc Lap Dong Minh, more commonly known as the Vietminh. Ho organized a guerrilla army that harassed the Japanese while he desperately tried to cultivate a friendship with the Americans. He was determined to prevent the French from returning to Vietnam and ruling his country. Ho was keenly aware that General Charles de Gaulle, who would become France's political leader after the war, was equally determined to reclaim the country for France once the war ended.

In 1945, Japan surrendered and Vietnam was free. For many Vietnamese, among them Mrs. Le Thi Anh, who was a student of French culture at the time, the moment for independence had come. She said:

> *Like thousands of other students, I saw the opportunity to recover our national independence. I loved my French teachers and I owe much of what I am today to the French culture. It was the writings of the great French philosophers Rousseau and Voltaire that taught me the ideals of freedom and democracy, for which I later took arms against French colonial rule. I adored my French literature teacher. But after I joined the underground, I was ready to shoot her should she stand in the way of our struggle for national independence.*[2]

On September 2, in the city of Hanoi, Vietnam, Ho Chi Minh gave a major speech celebrating the defeat of Japan. He was almost sixty years old and had been in exile from his country for almost all his adult life. Alarmingly thin, sickly, and dressed simply in a khaki tunic and white sandals, he slowly mounted a wooden platform to address an audience of thousands of joyous people. In a frail voice, he read the following words, which would have astonished many Americans, had they been present:

> *We hold [to be self-evident] the truth that all men are created equal, that they are endowed by their Creator with certain inalienable rights, among them life, liberty and the pursuit of happiness.*[3]

The words were taken from the American Declaration of Independence. For Ho knew that the decisive battle was now to be fought between himself and the

26

French for the hearts and minds of America's leaders. If he won, Vietnam would be independent. If he lost, it meant that his people would sooner or later go to war with France.

The French were warned that it was foolish and dangerous to try to return to Vietnam as rulers. Bo Dai, whom the French would install as Vietnam's puppet emperor, was perceptive enough, despite his weak character, to warn de Gaulle of the folly of reoccupying Vietnam:

> *You would better understand if you could see what is happening here, if you could feel this yearning for independence that is in everybody's heart, and which no human force can any longer restrain. Should you re-establish a French administration here, it will not be obeyed. Every village will be a nest of resistance, each former collaborator, an enemy, and your officials and colonists will themselves wish to leave this atmosphere which will choke them.*[4]

The French were not interested in Bo Dai's advice. Supported by England and America, they began to reassert their control over the country. On September 22, 1945, 1,400 French soldiers went on a rampage. They killed Vietnam sentries, kicked out members of the Vietminh government, took over police stations, and indiscriminately beat Vietnamese men, women, and children in their homes and shops. The Vietnamese struck back. They called a general strike. Then a group of Vietnamese massacred 150 French and Eurasian men, women, and children, and mutilated hundreds of others. The French retaliated by sending troops back into Vietnam. By December, the French had established a strong military presence in Vietnam and had won several bitterly fought battles around Saigon and Hanoi. The conflict was now between regular French military forces and smaller groups of well-trained, disciplined Vietminh troops whose specialty was hit-and-run raids and ambushes rather than prolonged battles.

The French, aware of the mounting pressures against colonial rule throughout Vietnam and the rest of the world, tried to provide the shadow of independence without the substance. They pressured Bo Dai to become emperor and proclaimed Vietnam independent, subject to French economic, political, and military control. France maintained its grip on the Army, all major industry, banks, imports and exports, and currency control. They also persuaded the United States to contribute substantial financial aid to help support their military effort. America thus became involved in Vietnam. The decisions that America made in the early 1950s would have fatal consequences in the 1960s.

Why did the United States agree to become involved in a foreign war that was of little use to it? The answer was the Cold War. Communism was the enemy, no matter what form it took. Since the end of World War II, the United States and the Soviet Union had been on a collision course. Fear and hatred of communism obsessed America's political leaders and motivated its foreign policy. This intolerance was intensified by the defeat in 1949 of the American-backed, corrupt Nationalist Chinese government of Generalissimo Chiang Kai-shek by the Chinese communists under the leadership of Mao Tse-tung. The following year, another collision occurred between America and communism when communist North Korea invaded South Korea. The United States, under the umbrella of the United Nations, sent troops to defend South Korea and stop communism. The conflict almost resulted in a nuclear war between the United States and China before it ended in a stalemate.

The French saw America's struggle against communism as an opportunity to press for American financial and military support in France's war in Vietnam. They argued that Ho Chi Minh and the Vietminh were part of a vast communist conspiracy to take over Asia. France, they claimed, was one of the last lines of defense against this menace. They met with sympathetic listeners. Dean Rusk, the assistant secretary of state for Far Eastern affairs, summed up the American position:

> . . . this isn't a civil war in the usual sense . . . it's an international war. . . . We have to look at it in terms of which side we are on in this kind of a struggle. . . . Because Ho Chi Minh is tied in with the Politburo, our policy is to support Bo Dai and the French in Indochina . . .[5]

Some American officials had the foresight to foresee what such an involvement would mean. Raymond Fosdick, a Far Eastern affairs expert with the U.S. State Department, noted in a memo:

> Ho Chi Minh as an alternative is decidedly unpleasant but . . . there may be unpredictable and unforeseen factors in this situation that may be more favorable to us than now seems probable. . . . Whether the French like it or not, independence is coming to Indochina. Why, therefore, do we tie ourselves to the tail of their battered kite. . . ?[6]

But the United States was not in the mood for rational thinking in Vietnam. The communist victory in China made large scale military aid to the French seem even more urgent in America's eyes. The Chinese could now supply the Vietminh Army with sophisticated military equipment, from weapons to trucks. They could also supply battle-experienced military advisers who had fought both guerrilla and conventional wars. America began to provide France with money and military supplies for its fight against Ho Chi Minh and the Vietminh Army. Now there was no question that the outcome of Vietnam would be settled on the battlefield.

Ho Chi Minh called it a battle between "the elephant and the grasshopper." He pointed out that the Vietnamese grasshopper would have to hop around to avoid being crushed by the French elephant's foot. They began to harass the French with hit-and-run tactics to keep them pinned down. The French generals, confident because they had more men and weapons than their enemy, made the same fatal mistake that the American Army would make a decade later. They failed to take into account the dedication of the Vietnamese soldiers. Calling themselves *chien si,* "fighters," they were willing to endure extreme physical hardships and sacrifice everything—including their lives—to free their country. Ho Chi Minh warned the French: "You can kill ten of my men for every one of yours. But even at these odds, you will lose and I will win."

Gradually, the Vietnamese began to increase the size of their operations. They began to build a formidable army to replace the guerrilla forces. One by one, they isolated and then destroyed French garrisons, killing and capturing their troops and ambushing reinforcements. Year after year, the struggle continued with no end in sight. By 1952 the French casualties had reached 90,000 dead, wounded, missing, and captured. In France itself, there was mounting opposition to what was called *la sale guerre,* "the dirty war." But the French persisted, despite mounting evidence that they could not win.

It was at this point that the French commanding general, Henry Navarre, decided to establish a base near the Laotian border at a village called Dien Bien Phu, despite warnings from his staff that he was putting his men into a "meat grinder" in which they would be crushed. In November 1953 the French dropped paratroopers into the area because there were no roads over which to transport troops. Giap, the Vietnamese commander, was overjoyed. The French had played right into his hands. They were now completely isolated in a valley surrounded by mountains. "We decided to wipe out at all

French paratroopers defending their base at
Dien Bien Phu in its last days. The base,
isolated in a valley surrounded by mountains,
fell to the Vietminh.

costs the whole enemy force at Dien Bien Phu," Giap
wrote after the battle.

General Navarre had deluded himself into believing
that Giap did not have the military strength to mount a
serious attack or position artillery in the mountains to
threaten the French fort. Navarre believed that his own
position, well fortified with artillery, was invincible and
could be reinforced by air strikes if necessary. The French
general was wrong on every count. Giap was able to
move his army of 70,000 men into the region despite

obstacles because of the dedication of his men. Cao Xuan Nghia, a *chien si* who fought at Dien Bien Phu, remembered how he and others suffered to reach the fort:

> We had to cross mountains and jungles, marching at night and sleeping by day to avoid enemy bombing. We sometimes slept in foxholes or just on the trail. We each carried a rifle, ammunition and hand grenades, and our packs contained a blanket, a mosquito net and a change of clothes. We each had a week's supply of rice, which we refilled at depots along the way. We ate greens and bamboo shoots that we picked in the jungle, and occasionally villagers would give us a bit of meat.[7]

On the other hand, the French army was becoming increasingly demoralized. Sergeant Guy de Chaumont-Guitry, who was twenty-four years old and destined to die in Vietnam, wrote in his diary:

> There are times we are so discouraged that we wish we could abandon the whole thing. The outposts are always being attacked, the roads are always being cut, the convoys always have to be escorted everywhere, assaults on anyone who becomes isolated, shots in all directions each evening. . . .[8]

By the spring of 1954, Giap was ready for a major offensive. His soldiers outnumbered the French by a ratio of five to one. Colonel Charles Piroth, the French officer in charge of artillery, boasted, "No Vietminh cannon will be able to fire three rounds before being destroyed by my artillery." He then watched helplessly as the Vietminh destroyed two of his three artillery positions within days. "I am completely dishonored,"[9] he told his friends. The next day Piroth took his life by placing a grenade in his teeth and pulling out the safety pin.

Even the weather favored the Vietminh. Clouds made it impossible for French aircraft to bomb Vietnamese positions or parachute supplies or reinforcements. Instead of launching an all-out attack, the Vietnamese wore down the French defenses, destroying them one by one until finally they surrendered. For a brief moment, it seemed possible that the United States might send air strikes to aid the French, and there was even talk of using atomic weapons. But in the end, everybody decided it was best to negotiate a solution. It was a time when world conflicts were winding down. Stalin had died, and the new leadership in Russia seemed willing to cooperate with the United States. A truce had been negotiated in Korea ending the fighting. And France wanted peace as much as Ho Chi Minh did. Both sides had suffered enormous casualties. Over 400,000 people had been killed, wounded, or captured in the seven years of fighting. America was reluctant to see the war end but saw no other choice and resigned itself to living with communism.

The peace conference took place during the spring of 1954. Among those attending were England, France, the Soviet Union, China, the United States and the Vietnamese. France, although defeated, still had troops in Vietnam and controlled the southern half of the country. Ho Chi Minh had expected that France would completely withdraw and leave the Vietnamese to work out their own political solutions. And he assumed that China, which had aided Vietnam in its victory, would support him in achieving that goal. This was not to happen, for China had no intention of seeing Vietnam unified. China did not want a strong country on its border, one that might someday prove a threat to its own interests. And without China supporting him at the peace table, Ho Chi Minh could not get the settlement he wanted. Frustrated, he came to the conclusion that his country stood alone and would have to depend on itself.

All Ho Chi Minh won was a cease-fire agreement and a promise that national elections would be held in two years to determine the political future of the country. Until then, Vietnam would be divided in half at the 17th parallel, with the Vietnamese under Ho controlling the North, and France and its allies allowed to retain a certain degree of control and influence in the South. As French troops withdrew from North Vietnam and Vietminh troops returned from the South, an uneasy truce hung over the land. Ngo Dinh Diem, the prime minister of South Vietnam, who would soon become its president, refused to accept the terms of the agreement. As far as he was concerned, there would be no elections. He had an ace up his sleeve, one which he would play in the coming years—the support of the United States. Diem predicted that soon there would be "another, more deadly war"[10] in Vietnam. He was to be proven tragically prophetic.

3

THE RADICALS
EMERGE

A s the year 1960 began, Vietnam was still a remote country, virtually unheard of by most Americans. College campuses throughout the United States seemed deceptively quiet. Clark Kerr, president of the University of California at Berkeley, surveyed the young people of America and remarked: "Employers are going to love this generation. . . . they are going to be easy to handle. There aren't going to be any riots."[1]

But beneath the seemingly calm surface, there were major social tremors that were about to shake many college campuses. Racism remained a major cancer in society. The Cold War dominated the hearts and minds of political and religious leaders. Crime was rising in the cities. There was also a growing number of young people in America. Fifteen percent of the population, some 27 million people, were between the ages of fourteen and twenty-one. Almost 4 million of them were in universities. A youth culture was beginning to develop that would soon seek its own identity.

On February 1, 1960, the calm was shattered when four freshmen from A&T College in Greensboro, North Carolina, sat down to have lunch at the counter of Woolworth's Five- and Ten-Cent Store in Greensboro. What was unusual about this act was that the lunch counter was segregated—it was for whites only—and the four students were black. Dave Richmond, one of the students, recalled how one of the first sit-ins came about:

> For about a week, we four fellows sat around the A&T campus talking about the integration movement. And we decided to go down to Woolworth's to see what would happen.[2]

From this small spark, a revolutionary fire exploded. Word of their actions raced first throughout North Carolina, then hit the rest of the South, and finally swept through the country. Sit-ins spread like brush fires all over the South. A spontaneous mass movement for civil rights began. Black and white students joined together to launch what was to be the most massive assault on segregation this country has ever seen. It was the American version of the Battle of Jericho. Like Joshua's army in biblical times, young people circled the walls of segregation and shouted "Freedom" until the walls came tumbling down. One anonymous white student explained why he joined the movement:

> I have never felt so intense, alive, with such a sense of well-being. . . . I have chosen to be outside of society after having been very much inside. I intend to fight that society which lied to and smothered me for so long and continues to do so to vast numbers of people. . . . I believe in freedom and must take the jump; I must take the chance of action.[3]

Tom Hayden was one of those whom the civil rights movement affected like an electric shock. Hayden grew up in the Royal Oak section of Michigan, twelve miles outside of Detroit. His childhood was like those of mil-

The civil rights movement attracted
tens of thousands of college students. For
many students, this would prove to be only
the beginning of their political activism.

lions of other American children in the 1950s. His parents
considered themselves good citizens who could never
imagine themselves demonstrating. Hayden himself was
a talented ballplayer, attended the Catholic church, and
was a good student. In high school, he was not aware of
the McCarthy hearings, the anticommunist crusades, or
the condition and treatment of blacks in the South. Like

most teenagers, he planned to finish high school, go to college, get married, and find a job. Yet, despite his "normality," he was somewhat nonconformist, but his restlessness was without focus.

When Hayden was a freshman at the University of Michigan, most student demonstrations on American campuses were limited to panty raids on women's dormitories by fraternities. A few universities, such as Berkeley, had begun to show increasing political awareness in the late fifties. The University of Michigan also had a small group of activists. Al Haber, a friend of Hayden's there, formed a small organization that would be destined to play a major role in the antiwar movement during the next decade. It was called the SDS, the Students for a Democratic Society, and it was created out of the ashes of an old socialistic labor political organization known as the SLID, the Student League for Industrial Democracy. The SLID was the first student organization in America, but by the late 1950s it had become a relic of the past. Haber gave it new life by converting it to SDS. The timing was right. One year after the new organization was formed, the civil rights movement began.

The civil rights movement would become the crucible in which the antiwar movement was formed. Hayden, like many other students, came to political action gradually. The heady early days of the sit-ins gave way to the violent struggles of the sixties. The South would not abandon segregation without a fight. Nonviolent civil rights protesters and organizers faced violent opposition in Mississippi, Alabama, and Georgia. Protesters were beaten, jailed, shot at, and sometimes murdered. Hayden—who had become editor of *The Daily,* the university's campus newspaper, which had a great influence in universities throughout America—felt a growing desire to become a participant. "As many thousands of Southern students were arrested and many beaten, my respect and identification with their courage and conviction deepened," he wrote. The turning point for Hayden came at a conference attended by young black and white students from SNCC, the Student Nonviolent Coordinating Committee, which was spearheading the drive to break down segregation in the South:

> . . . a key to my own transformation was the presence of about twenty-five representatives of the Student Nonviolent Coordinating Committee (SNCC), the students fresh from beatings and jail. They were in many ways like myself—young, politically innocent, driven by moral values, impatient with their elders, risking their "lives, their fortune and their sacred honor"—in short, a genuine revolutionary leadership.
>
> They lived on a fuller level of feeling than any people I have ever seen; partly because they were making modern history and partly by risking death, they came to know the value of living each moment to the fullest. . . . Here were the models of the charismatic commitment I was seeking—I wanted to live like them.[4]

In November 1960, as the civil rights movement spread throughout the South, John F. Kennedy was narrowly elected president of the United States. Many saw in the young president a shining incarnation of the youthful spirit of America. His personal charm and idealism seemed to promise the beginning of a golden age in American life, one in which the dark days of McCarthyism and the Cold War would be overcome and an era of peace ushered in. For those young Americans who wanted America to fulfill the promises of the Declaration of Independence and the Constitution, Kennedy seemed to be the perfect president. He promised change, he was optimistic and progressive, and he appeared willing to work for world peace. When, in his inauguration speech,

Kennedy said, ". . . ask not what your country can do for you; ask what you can do for your country," his words struck a responsive chord in the hearts of many young people. Those engaged in the struggle for civil rights believed they had a leader who would champion their cause.

Tragically, it was not to be. Students involved in the civil rights movement turned to the Kennedy administration for protection and support in the South, but the administration was not responsive. Kennedy was unwilling to challenge Southern political power. Robert Kennedy, the United States attorney general and the president's brother, seldom took direct action against those who were violating the civil rights of protesters. FBI agents, often friendly with local Southern peace officers, stood idly by as civil rights activists were illegally arrested or beaten on federal property, a clear violation of the law.

Part of the problem was that Kennedy had more to worry about than civil rights. His attempt to overthrow Fidel Castro, the communist president of Cuba, by supporting an anti-Castro Cuban armed invasion of the island, had met with disaster and defeat. Nikita Khrushchev, then head of the Soviet Union, had bullied him at a summit conference. And in Vietnam, a country that most Americans had still not heard of, Ngo Dinh Diem, the president of South Vietnam, was slowly dragging America into a war.

In 1957, Diem, then prime minister of South Vietnam, had driven out Bo Dai as leader of South Vietnam and, with American help, had crushed opposition to his regime and become president. Although Diem was supposed to hold elections to unify Vietnam, he had no intention of doing so. Diem knew, as President Eisenhower had noted in his diary, that if the elections had been held, Ho Chi Minh would have received "eighty percent of the vote."

Instead, Diem began to launch a campaign of terror

against former communists and noncommunists who had fought with the Vietminh against the French. He uprooted farmers from their land, turned villages into military zones in which his soldiers abused the people, and made no significant economic reforms. He used American aid to increase the personal fortunes of himself and his family, and to build up a military force that would protect him from being overthrown. While many United States advisers were privately upset with Diem, they publicly supported him—there was no one else. Diem knew this, and while he took $1 billion of American money, he did whatever he wanted. One American officer characterized him "as a puppet, but a puppet who pulls his own strings."

Ho Chi Minh watched what was happening to the South. He knew that if he wanted to unify Vietnam he would have to do so by war. He felt the Vietnamese communist guerrillas in the South were not strong enough to resist, and he ordered them not to revolt. But the Vietminh, the South Vietnamese communists, now called Vietcong by Diem, were forced to take matters into their own hands. They had little choice. If they did not strike back, they would be crushed. Out of 6,000 members who returned to the South after the truce with France had been signed, only some 2,500 were left. Ho finally had to approve their struggle. In December 1960 the newly elected president of the United States was greeted with the announcement of a new organization in South Vietnam, the National Liberation Front. It was a broad-based anti-Diem coalition, run by communists but containing a number of noncommunists.

President Kennedy was determined to stop communism in Vietnam. In part, this was because he felt he had to project an image of toughness to the world. He did not want to be perceived as weak. In an interview in *The New York Times,* he was quoted as saying, "Now we have a problem in making our power credible. Vietnam is the place." The president's brother, Robert, looked forward to the coming conflict and predicted with great confidence, "Within two years we are going to win."[5]

The U.S. military had advised the new president that all the South Vietnamese needed to defeat the communists was American military training and plenty of the latest equipment. The training was supplied by American advisers, military men who went to Vietnam to teach the Vietnamese Army how to fight but who were not supposed to fight themselves. Before Kennedy was elected, there were 700 military advisers in Vietnam. The military asked Kennedy for several thousand more. He agreed. His under secretary of state George Ball warned him that his policy would one day lead to 300,000 men being sent to Vietnam. Kennedy replied: ". . . you're crazy as hell, George. That will never happen."[6] Shortly afterward, American helicopter pilots began to fly raids against Vietminh positions in the South and carry South Vietnamese troops into battle. Within two years, 16,000 American advisers would be poured into the country to assist the South Vietnamese in turning back the tide of communism. Anne Miller, then a writer with the U.S. Information Service, was working in Vietnam when Kennedy decided to escalate:

> At the outset, we had a minimum of military men there. And all of them were working on village projects, not only military training, because the most important thing was to try to teach the Vietnamese army not only how to defend itself, but how to be accepted by the village.
>
> I could not believe it when Kennedy announced he was going to send in regular troops. That was the beginning of the end.[7]

Caught between growing war in Vietnam and the increasing violence against civil rights workers in America, Kennedy was under tremendous pressure. In South Vietnam, the communists were terrorizing the American-trained South Vietnamese Army, called the ARVN. They assassinated officials, raided and attacked army units, and controlled many villages and towns in the South. At the same time, in the American South, segregationists were terrorizing civil rights workers and those who supported them. SNCC's attempt to organize voter registration drives and integrate schools and public transportation so infuriated southern whites that they turned to violence. There were shootings, bombings, beatings, and mass arrests of civil rights workers.

Tom Hayden not only documented what was happening in the South, but he himself was beaten and imprisoned. Later he would testify before a commission investigating the causes of violence:

> *Working in the South brought us face-to-face with the reality that we had never known, the direct reality of the police state. . . . The crucial discovery of that experience for many students was that the South was not an isolated or backward region but an integral part of the whole country. . . . An elementary lesson began to dawn on us . . . and that lesson was simply that law serves power.*[8]

That discovery led to a major decision by Hayden and a number of white students that the time had come to act. They decided to organize a national student movement that would mobilize America's youth in support of SNCC and the civil rights movement. The vehicle for action would be SDS—the Students for a Democratic Society. An SDS convention was called in June 1962 at Port Huron, Michigan, and a variety of representatives from student organizations were invited. The purpose was to form a broad coalition of students from different groups who would commit themselves to work for peace, civil rights, and the labor movement. The convention not only produced a sense of unity; it also produced a manifesto that had considerable influence among a whole generation of students. Known as the Port Huron Statement, its opening paragraph began:

> *We are people of this generation, bred in at least modern comfort, housed now in universities, looking uncomfortably at the world we inherit. . . .*[9]

The manifesto noted the contradiction between the Declaration of Independence and racism, between the call for peace by government officials and the huge military budget, between automation and the unemployment it created, and between wealth and poverty. It committed SDS to resolving these contradictions by making the ideals of America a reality.

The Port Huron Statement spelled out the dreams, hopes, and programs for a generation determined to influence the world in a moral way. It was a spiritual doctrine rather than a political one. It expressed hope that determined people could change America through the use of moral rather than physical force. The statement was one of the high points of the idealism of the sixties. One student recalled the impact the Port Huron convention had on him this way:

> *The thing I was thinking about was what was I going to do with my life. . . . I wanted to learn, I wanted to learn how America was organized and I wanted to find out about myself. Another thing I felt about myself was the ideology of the alienated: "The Old values have been destroyed; the old structures and institutions of the past no longer fit our needs. Therefore we must rebuild."*[10]

"It was the beginning of a journey," Bob Ross, one of the participants, noted.[11] Soon, the journey would lead to a deep and bitter conflict throughout the land.

4

A CHIEN SI
IS BORN

In a small Vietnamese village then called Ky La, near Da Nang in central Vietnam, a twelve-year-old girl was also making a spiritual journey, one that had begun in early childhood.

Le Ly had never heard of Elvis Presley. Rock and roll was music from another planet as far as she was concerned. She was, in her own words, "a peasant," a daughter of a family of farmers whose life centered around the planting and harvesting of rice. Even when she was a small child, Le Ly's father had instilled in her pride in her country and the necessity of fighting for its freedom from foreign rule:

> My father taught me to love God, my family, our traditions and the people we could not see: our ancestors. He taught me that to sacrifice one's self for freedom . . . in the manner of our women warriors, including Miss Triung Nhi Trung Trac, who drowned herself rather than give in to foreign conquerors, was a very high honor.[1]

It was the dream of many Vietnamese children growing up in the 1950s in Vietnam to one day become *chien si*—fighters for their country's freedom.

Before the arrival of the Americans in Vietnam, life for most villagers centered around the rice fields rather than the battlefield. During the planting seasons in May and October, Vietnamese families worked in the fields fourteen hours a day preparing the ground for the rice crop. The rice would be planted in a nursery until it grew into stalks. Then the stalks would be pulled up and planted into rice paddies. Transplanting the rice stalks was the task of women and children. Hour after hour, they would bend in knee-deep muddy water planting the rice. When the planting was finished, the fields had to be fertilized and weeded. Weeding was another difficult job traditionally carried out by women and children. For fourteen hours a day over a period of several weeks, the weeders worked, bending over in water that attracted mosquitoes, snakes, leeches, and crabs. Thus, weeding was dangerous as well as unpleasant.

During Le Ly's early childhood, the war with France was still raging. Her family actively supported the Vietminh against the French. Le Ly's sister prepared rice balls and bandages for the soldiers who were fighting. Her parents smuggled supplies to the Vietminh soldiers through underground tunnels. Le Ly became aware of the war at a young age through the songs of peace and freedom her mother taught her:

> *We love the words* hoa binh;
> Hoa binh *means peace—first* hoa, *then* binh.
> Hoa *means "together" and* binh *means "all the same."*
> *When we're all together, no one is parted.*
> *When we're all the same, no one is at war.*
> *Peace means no more suffering.*
> Hoa Binh *means no more war.*[2]

Life for most Vietnamese villagers revolved around
long days in the rice fields. Here, a Vietnamese
farmer plowed a village field with a water buffalo.

Her older sisters used to sing and dance to entertain the Vietminh soldiers. Le Ly remembered one song her sister sang contained the verses:

Remember—a young boy growing up
Has seen his fatherland suffer.
Because of that I will be brave!
I will lead the valiant. . . .
With bare hands we destroy the enemy!
Central citizens resisting the French![3]

Le Ly was three years old when she first encountered French soldiers. To her child's mind at the time, the French and their airplanes seemed to her like snakes and monsters out of a nightmarish fairy tale:

Once, we were playing . . . when people began to scream and thunder broke from a sunny sky. The ground shook as in an earthquake, and giant snakes with heads coughed loudly. I knew they were giants because they were so loud. The snake's spittle flew into the village and covered the people with blood. . . . Sometimes, the snakes' keepers would be in the village. They were giant men who smelled bad because they were big and sweaty and often had to crawl through piles of dung. They had long noses, round eyes and wore funny hats. . . . In every way, they resembled the demons in our stories. . . . They had long teeth, horns, faces like horses or boars, and made the noise of fire or dragons. Even the friendly ones made us sick with horror.[4]

The end of the war with France brought some relief to Le Ly's village. But it was not to last. Several years after the truce between North Vietnam and France was signed, Diem began his campaign to hunt down and kill all Vietminh living in the South. At the same time, Diem and his sister-in-law Madame Ngo Dinh Nhu (the wife of Diem's brother, who was head of internal security) began an intensive propaganda campaign, at the urging of their American advisers, to win the "hearts and minds" of the Vietnamese farmers. Madame Nhu organized children and women into the Phu Nu Cong Hoa, "women warriors," who were supposed to drive away the Vietcong terrorists. Le Ly and other children were taught patriotic songs, how to shoot with a rifle (which was taken away from Le Ly after she learned how to use it), and how to keep themselves safe from the Vietcong. South Vietnamese soldiers began to frequent the village and flirt with Le Ly. It all seemed like a game until one night, as she was looking out her window, she saw some strange men quickly enter a neighbor's house, a man by the name of Manh, and drive him and his friends out:

> Manh was the last one out, led at gunpoint with his hands on top of his head. I could hear his familiar voice arguing with the strangers. "But I don't know what you're talking about" and "Why? Who told you that?" . . . Suddenly one of the strangers barked an order . . . and two of his comrades prodded Manh to the edge of the road. I could still hear Manh begging for his life when two rifle shots cut him short. The strangers then ran a Viet Cong flag up the pole that stood outside the schoolhouse and left as quickly as they had come. The leader shouted over his shoulder: Anyone who touches that flag will get the same thing as that traitor!"[5]

Manh was a follower of President Diem and was condemned to death as a traitor by the Vietcong. After his execution, the South Vietnamese soldiers returned to the village in force and built defenses around it. Then they waited for the Vietcong to return. They told everyone to stay inside, and they set up ambushes around the village, listening for the dogs to bark to warn them when strangers approached. But the Vietcong did not fall into the trap, and the soldiers left. Immediately after that, the Vietcong returned. They destroyed all the fortifications the Republican soldiers had constructed and took two more men outside the village limits and shot them. One of the men had been an informer. Le Ly was surprised at her own feelings about his execution:

> I felt deep in my young girl's heart that he had gotten what he . . . deserved and I found that revenge . . . tasted sweeter than I expected. It made even a puny farm girl feel like someone important.[6]

Before they left, the Vietcong ordered the villagers to send their dogs away. It seemed like a strange command. The next day, the Republican soldiers returned and began a house-to-house search looking for Vietcong sympathizers. For the first time, soldiers began to stay overnight in the village. They took food from the villagers without paying for it. One night, as Le Ly was having a nightmare about ghosts, she was suddenly awakened by her father putting his hand over her face. He whispered for her to keep still. In the morning, Le Ly discovered that the Republican soldiers had suddenly withdrawn in terror:

> . . . word passed out quickly that a half-dozen Republicans had been murdered in their sleep— throats cut from ear to ear. "The dogs—where are the dogs?" I heard a Republican officer cry in dismay. He wondered what had happened to the watchdogs of Ky La.[7]

The killings created a classic situation that was taking place throughout South Vietnam. By day, the South Vietnamese Army would control the villages and nearby roads. By night, the Vietcong would rule. Now Le Ly and the other children were to receive an education in war.

They were taught how to set up booby traps and decoys by moonlight or by oil lamps. These included cartridge traps, which were bullets held over a nail that discharged when you stepped on them; punji pits, which were spiked boards set knee-deep in the ground that broke in half and sent poison barbs into a soldier's legs when he stepped on them; and a variety of trip-wire grenade traps. Le Ly and the others helped to set these traps on paths used by Republican soldiers.

> . . . although we knew how deadly these traps could be, we kids had no second thoughts about helping the Viet Cong make them or put them in place. To us, war was still a game and "our enemy," we were assured, deserved everything bad that happened to them.[8]

Part of the children's education was ideological. Special schools were set up at night and Viet Cong cadre leaders instructed the boys and girls. The children learned who Ho Chi Minh was and sang songs in his honor. They learned what they were expected to do for their village, their families, and the revolution. They were instructed in the difference between the liberation soldiers of the Vietcong and the Republicans and their newly arriving American allies, whom many of the children had heard about but had not yet seen. The children were taught that the Americans were there to keep the Vietnamese people divided and to deny them their rights to be free and unified. To achieve their independence, the Vietnamese had to wage war until the Americans were defeated. The young people were told stories in which Vietnamese children sacrificed their lives for their country, like the boy

During the early years of the war, Vietnamese
classrooms were used to instruct students
in ideological issues. Students were taught
what they were expected to do for their
country in order to win the war.

who stuck his head into an enemy cannon so his comrades could capture it. Le Ly remembered how one night
her cadre instructor told them:

> *The imperialists and their running dogs have aircraft*
> *and bombs and long-range artillery and ten men for*
> *every one of ours. We have only rags and rifles and*

those supplies we carry on our backs. When the
Republicans and the Americans come to your vil-
lage, they trample your crops, burn your houses
and kill your relatives just for getting in the way. We
respect your homes and the shrines of your ances-
tors and execute only those who are traitors to our
cause. President Diem gives you foreign invaders
while Ho Chi Minh promises you a free Vietnam.
The Republicans fight for pay, like mercenaries,
while we fight only for your independence.[9]

Le Ly's instructors taught the children a song about
the Americans which ran in part:

Americans come to kill our people.
Follow America and kill your relatives!
The smart bird flies before it is caught. . . .
Follow us, and you'll always have a family.
Follow America and you'll always be alone![10]

Even though Le Ly and the other children were
aware of the ideological nature of their instruction, they
also recognized there was a good deal of truth in what
was said. The Americans and the Republican soldiers
often treated them with contempt or bullied them. The
Republicans often stole food or took it without paying,
and they sometimes raped women. By contrast, the Vietcong acted more like neighbors. They did not insult the
people of Le Ly's village. They paid for what they took
and treated the people with respect. Yet, they could be
cruel and vindictive, quick to judge and punish—without
benefit of a fair and impartial trial—those they felt were
aiding the other side. As the war grew longer and more
bitter, the Vietcong did commit atrocities. But in the beginning, Le Ly and the other children of the village looked
upon them as their friends and heroes. In their war games,
everybody wanted to be a Vietcong *chien si,* and those

who agreed to play the Republicans or Americans did so reluctantly.

The Vietcong often instructed the children how they could help their cause through a series of questions and answers. The cadre leader would ask the question and reward the children with praise when they gave the right answer.

> "What will you do when the enemy sleeps in your house?" the cadre leader asked.
> "Steal his weapons," we answered in chorus.
> "Steal his medicine! Steal his food."
> "And what will you do with what you steal?"
> "Give it to you!"[11]

Le Ly and her playmates became expert thieves. They stole weapons, hand grenades, and, most importantly, first aid kits—the Vietcong guerrillas lacked medicine to treat their wounds. The children were also encouraged to steal toothpaste, soap, and cigarettes. Le Ly once stole a hand grenade and hid it in a rice container that held fruit that looked like pineapples. Her father accidentally picked up the grenade while looking for a piece of fruit to eat and scolded Le Ly for taking such chances; he buried the grenade. Le Ly went and stole another. Later on, her thoughtlessness struck her:

> The fact that these might lead to deaths on both sides, including women and children, never occurred to us. For us, the new war was a game for earning medals and an honored place on lists.[12]

Every so often, a child would get caught. A friend of Le Ly's named Thi tried to steal a machine gun and was caught when soldiers found her struggling with a box of heavy ammunition. She disappeared and was never heard from again. The Vietcong were concerned about children being captured and instructed them to hide if they were in danger of being caught. If it was impossible to hide, then they were to commit suicide, taking as many of the enemy as possible with them. By dying in battle, the Vietcong leaders told them, they would become heroes. The reality, as Le Ly later learned, was that the Vietcong preferred the children to be killed rather than captured and tortured to reveal their secrets. But in the early years, Le Ly was caught up in the war. It had become an insatiable dragon that roared around Ky La.

One day, as Le Ly was tending water buffalo in a field, she heard the sound of a strange motor she had never heard before:

> *Like a tiger growling in a cave, the hollow noise became a roar and our buffalo grunted and trotted without prodding toward the trees. Steadily, the roar increased and I looked into the sun to see two helicopters, whining and flapping like furious birds, settle out of the sky towards me. The wind whipped my clothes and snatched the sun hat from my head. What could a puny girl do but fall down on her knees and hold fast to mother earth.*
>
> *To my surprise, I did not die. . . . As I raised my eyes, the dull green door on the side of the ship slid open and the most splendid man I had ever seen stepped onto the marshy ground. He was a giant . . . crispy clean in starched fatigues with a yellow scarf tucked into his shirt and a golden patch on his shoulder.*
>
> *Still cowering, I watched his brawny blond-haired hands raise binoculars to his eyes. He scanned the tree line around Ky La, ignoring me completely. . . . He said something in his queer language to another fair-skinned soldier inside the door . . . and then climbed back into his machine.*
>
> *Instantly, the flap-flap-flap and siren howl in-*

creased. . . . As if plucked by the hand of God, the enormous green machine tiptoed on its skids and swooped away, climbing steadily toward the treetops. In seconds, the hollow growl was gone. . . .[13]

It was Le Ly's first encounter with the American soldiers in Vietnam. It would not be the last for either herself or her people.

5
1963

The American Army had no better soldier to send to Vietnam to help train the South Vietnamese Army than Lieutenant Colonel John Vann. He was tough, bright, inventive, a realist, and fearless in battle. Best of all, he believed in the military and moral superiority of the United States military. When he arrived in Vietnam in 1962 to advise a South Vietnam army commander on how to defeat the Vietcong in his area, it seemed to Vann that his destiny was calling.

John Vann believed in the righteousness of the American cause in Vietnam. He believed that communism was an evil system and that it was America's duty to save the Vietnamese people. Like most Americans sent to Vietnam, Vann was unaware of or indifferent to Vietnamese history. He also supported President Kennedy's policy to train the South Vietnamese to win the war themselves rather than have American soldiers fight their battles for them. It was a tough job, as one of Vann's colleagues, Colonel Chuck Allen, discovered:

> *Being an advisor was a very difficult position. . . . It takes a while to learn that the American way isn't*

In the early 1960s, American "advisers" were
sent to Vietnam to help train the South
Vietnamese Army. Although the Americans
initially felt that the war could be won, the
program proved to be a dismal failure.

always right when dealing with a foreign army. In Vietnam, the poor bastards had been at war for fifteen years. . . . And here we come . . . wanting to win the war in six months. [1]

When Vann arrived in the North Mekong Delta, the Vietcong controlled the region. Vann was determined to change that. He realized that the South Vietnamese Army was not very eager to fight. Their officers did not like to engage in battle with the Vietcong. They refused to leave camp, go out on night patrols, or seek out the enemy forces. Whenever Vann set up an ambush, the South Vietnamese soldiers would inevitably let the enemy know of their presence by coughing, talking, or making noise to attract attention.

Eventually, Vann began to have some success with his Vietnamese troops. By using American helicopters, with their awesome fire power, as well as other sophisticated weapons, the South Vietnamese Army began to inflict heavy casualties on the Vietcong. Vann felt that if his troops could win a major battle, the tide would turn against the Vietnamese communists and give the South Vietnamese Army the confidence it needed. Vann wanted to fight a large Vietcong force, but he felt he had little chance of doing so. The Vietcong was a guerrilla force, and large battles were not their way of fighting. John Vann should have remembered the saying "The only thing worse than not having your wishes come true is having them come true."

At dawn on January 2, 1963, Vann's force was carried by helicopter to the small village of Tan Thoi; he believed this was a Vietcong headquarters. Nearby was the village of Bac, which Americans called Ap Bac, *ap* being the Vietnamese word for "village" or "hamlet." Intelligence reports estimated the number of Vietcong there at 129. There were three times that number present. Still, the South Vietnamese had over 1,400 men plus artillery, helicopters, and fighter bombers. Vann believed that the battle which he had longed for was finally about to happen and that it would be one-sided. Unfortunately for Vann and the South Vietnamese, it turned out to be as one-sided as the battle Goliath fought with David.

The South Vietnamese Army had expected the Vietcong to run away when they saw they were outgunned and outnumbered. Then they could be shot down from the air by helicopters. Instead, the Vietcong dug in and fought back. They fought coolly and calmly, making every bullet count. The South Vietnamese had superior rifles and machine guns, as well as artillery, napalm, bombs, gunships, and armored vehicles equipped with flame throwers—which the Vietcong feared—yet all these weapons proved useless. As a result of the incompetence and cowardice of the South Vietnamese officers, and the fierce courage and determination of the Vietcong, the one-sided battle ended with the victory of the underdogs. The Vietcong killed eighty South Vietnamese soldiers and wounded 100 others. They also killed three American advisers and wounded eight, and shot down five helicopters. In turn, they suffered only eighteen killed and thirty-five wounded.

Ironically, the South Vietnamese Army claimed the battle as a great military victory because the Vietcong eventually retreated after the fighting. And while John Vann publicly supported the army's version of the battle, he knew it had been a major defeat. He sat down and wrote his report of the battle, bluntly telling his superiors that the South Vietnamese Army could not hold South Vietnam for the United States. After receiving this report, Vann's commanding officer, General Paul Harkin, in charge of American operations in Vietnam, completely ignored it and publicly predicted that the South Vietnamese Army would have the Vietcong on the run in "one year." His boss, Secretary of Defense Robert McNamara, was not quite so optimistic, but also believed in America's ultimate victory: "We must take a conservative view and assume it will take three years instead of one year."[2] In any case, as McNamara was to say later on, he could see "light at the end of the tunnel."

Part of the problem was that the Americans could not see things from a Vietnamese perspective. Lu Mong Lang remembered that when he met his first American adviser, he used sign language to communicate. Yet, he was looking forward to working with Americans, whom he admired greatly:

> The Vietnamese word for "American" is My, which is also a synonym for what is beautiful. When I was twenty years old, if I wore a nice belt, people would say, "The belt looks very American." Anything that looked nice we would say, "That is very American.". . .
>
> But frankly, we did have a lot of conflict with the American advisors. Americans were victorious heroes after World War II, very proud of themselves. . . . It was our impression that American people looked down on those who did not speak English; on those people who did not have the same culture; on those people who are not good-looking . . . small, dark. So naturally, having a partner like that, we could not expect that the Americans would have full respect for us.[3]

As the American involvement in Vietnam grew, the slaughter of innocent civilians increased. In the spring of 1963, American bombers attacked the village of Man Quang where Le Ly's beloved aunt lived. The raid came at noon, a time when children were getting out of school. Her aunt's pregnant daughter-in-law was making lunch for her husband and for Aunt Thu's four grandchildren when the bombs began to fall. The family dived under the only wooden table in the house and everybody, including the children, sheltered the woman who was pregnant. Suddenly, a bomb landed in the front yard and its shrapnel ripped through the house, striking everyone except the daughter-in-law. Le Ly's aunt and one of the children were killed.

To the South Vietnamese, their situation was made even more difficult by the corruption and arrogance of President Diem and his family. In the countryside, farmers were uprooted from their homes and villages and sent to live in strategic hamlets where they would be "protected" from the Vietcong. In the cities, corruption flourished. Jan Barry, an American radio technician who was sent to South Vietnam to train the Vietnamese, was shocked to see how openly elections were rigged to favor the government so that it would "win" ninety-eight percent of the vote. He discovered that the police controlled the voting by clubbing or arresting those who disagreed with the government. Barry began to question the role of American soldiers there:

> With experiences like that, many of us began to
> realize that something was really wrong with what
> our purpose was there—being a trip-wire protection
> of this police state. We were there as bait. . . . If the
> ten or twelve thousand of us get overrun, we were
> the excuse for even a bigger war.[4]

When Barry returned to the United States after his tour of duty, he was shocked to discover that most of the military was completely unaware of what was happening in Vietnam. He was asked by high-ranking officers: "What have you been fighting in, son?" When he told them Vietnam, they would ask: "Where is that? We have people fighting over there?"[5] But American ignorance of Vietnam could not last forever. In the spring of 1963, Vietnam would suddenly dominate the headlines.

The trouble began when President Diem, who was

Catholic, forbade Buddhist priests from flying the Buddhist flag to celebrate the birthday of the founder of their religion, Siddhartha Gautama, known as Buddha. On May 8, 1963, the monks staged a peaceful protest against Diem's edict. A company of Diem's soldiers opened fire into the crowd, killing nine persons, including several children. One month later, the monks struck back in their own way.

One of the protesters was Quang Duc, sixty-six years old, who had been a Buddhist monk since he was fifteen. He was a deeply reverent man, devoutly committed to his religion, and he had been deeply offended at Diem's refusal to allow Buddhists to practice their religion freely. The slaughter of the peaceful protesters in May saddened him, and he decided to call attention to what was happening in Vietnam in the most dramatic way possible.

On a beautiful spring day in Vietnam, June 11, 1963, Quang Duc dressed himself in the traditional orange robe of a Buddhist priest. He was driven in a motorcade of other priests and nuns to a busy intersection in downtown Saigon. At the intersection, Quang Duc climbed out of the car and, crossing his legs, serenely sat down in the middle of the road as traffic passed by him. A few curious pedestrians stopped to watch the proceedings. Quickly, the other monks and nuns made a circle around him. As Quang Duc pressed his hands together in prayer, one of his fellow monks poured gasoline over him from a can while another set fire to him with a lighter. With a roar, the flames engulfed him. It was an astonishing sight. People watching the scene threw themselves to the ground in reverence. Traffic stopped. The flames leaped higher and higher as Quang Duc, his hands still folded in prayer, was totally consumed by fire until only his heart remained. By the following day, the flames would reach around the world.

Quang Duc's self-sacrifice was a gesture of protest, one which monks had traditionally used for centuries.

President Diem met with Buddhist monks to gain
their support. Diem, a Catholic, would not allow
Buddhists to practice their religion freely. Most monks
opposed Diem because of his religious intolerance.

Some of Quang Duc's fellow monks had offered to burn
themselves, but since he was the oldest, he was allowed
to be the first. His gesture was a protest against the corrupt, incompetent, and brutal South Vietnamese government led by Diem and his sister-in-law, Madame Nhu.
The government responded to the protest with biting cyn-
icism: Madame Nhu coldly told the press, "If the monks
want to have another barbecue, I will be glad to supply
the gasoline and the match."

For a brief moment, the picture of the burning monk combined with the U.S. presence there caught America's attention. But while most Americans were shocked, they were not yet aware of their nation's growing involvement in Vietnam. The energies of young idealists who would later form the core of the antiwar movement were still mobilized in the struggle for civil rights. While SNCC was growing increasingly unwilling to work with white students, young white militants were seeking their own battles against racism. SDS formed ERAP, the Economic Research Action Project, where students went into the slums and ghettos of various cities to organize poor blacks and whites against local political and legal oppression.

Meanwhile, President Kennedy, realizing there was no longer any possibility of working with President Diem in Vietnam, reluctantly gave permission to the Central Intelligence Agency to work with a dissident group of Vietnamese officers to overthrow the government. Kennedy wanted to establish a government that would be more cooperative with the United States and receptive to its advice. In November 1963 the Vietnamese generals involved overthrew Diem and took him and his brother Nhu prisoner. The officers who captured them promised that they would not be harmed but would be sent into exile. However, as soon as the captives were placed in the back of a military armored vehicle, they were gunned down. Kennedy was shocked. It was not what he had planned. The deaths of Diem and Nhu proved to be a foreshadowing of his own doom. Three weeks later, on November 22, 1963, he was assassinated while visiting Dallas, Texas. The country was plunged into mourning. Young people who saw Kennedy as the embodiment of youth felt his death had killed something within themselves.

Vice President Lyndon Johnson quickly assumed the presidency. Many considered him a political barbarian, and feared and hated him. Those fighting for civil rights feared that since Johnson was a Southerner (a Texan), he would use the power of his office to support the South in its efforts to suppress the civil rights movement. They were mistaken. Johnson turned out to be the best civil rights president since Abraham Lincoln. He saw with clarity that segregation was finished in the South. He outlined a war on poverty that, if successful, would go a long way to heal the racial divisions in America. Tragically however, he was blind to the fact that the corrupt military regimes in South Vietnam were also finished and that the destiny of this small Asian country lay with the rulers of the North. His failure to recognize this fundamental truth led him to plunge America into a bitter war. Tom Hayden remembered the consequences of this decision for civil rights:

> . . . there was a real promise of hope for the poor, both blacks and whites, through the poverty program. Then came the buildup in Vietnam and I watched the program broken and eviscerated. . . . I knew America would never invest the necessary funds or energies in rehabilitation of its poor so long as Vietnam continued to draw men and skills and money like some demonic destructive suction tube.[6]

6

RESISTANCE
AND WAR

On the evening of December 27, 1964, a small, seemingly nondescript, late-middle-aged man rose to address a group of SDS members in the meeting hall of the Cloakmakers Union in New York. His name was I. F. Stone and he was the publisher, editor, writer, and sole owner of a newsletter called *The Weekly,* which he had been publishing for almost ten years. *The Weekly* revealed the behind-the-scenes actions of the United States government, including many secret-operations activities, some of which were either unconstitutional or immoral. The paper's influence extended far beyond its small circulation.

The subject of discussion that December night was Vietnam and the growing American military presence there. Twenty-three thousand American military and civilian personnel were working to keep the corrupt and ineffective South Vietnamese government in power and defeat the National Liberation Front's efforts to overthrow the government. Stone explained to his generally uninformed audience the recent history of Vietnam as well as the dangers and possible consequences of America's involvement. He made clear his belief that America should withdraw immediately.

After Stone's address, SDS members then debated what their response to Vietnam should be. They finally agreed to stage a demonstration against the war on April 17, 1965. One of the arguments that some members made against the demonstration was that only a few thousand people at most would attend and that it would do little good and receive little public attention.

But an unforeseen event was to dramatically change the nature of the march. On the bitter-cold night of February 6, 1965, Specialist Fourth Class Jesse Pyle sat shivering in his trench. He was one of a number of guards posted around the U.S. military base near Pleiku in Vietnam. At two o'clock in the morning, a sudden noise startled him. When he went to investigate, he saw shadows crossing the defense perimeter. He began shooting. Suddenly, all hell broke loose. Mortar fire and automatic weapons exploded and men shouted and screamed. "We're going to die," one American shouted out. "We're all going to die."[1]

Eight Americans did die and a hundred others were wounded. Ten U.S. planes were destroyed. Upon receiving the news, Lyndon Johnson angrily told his advisers that he had had enough. He ordered the commencement of Operation Flaming Dart, followed by Operation Rolling Thunder. Both were bombing attacks of North Vietnam. In addition, Johnson began to increase the number of troops stationed there. Unofficially, America's large-scale involvement in the war was on.

Many Americans were shocked. They looked for a vehicle in which to express their protest and anger and saw that SDS was already ahead of them. Suddenly, the small demonstration became a major event. On April 17, instead of the originally estimated two to three thousand marchers, over 15,000 people showed up. The issues

President Lyndon Johnson escalated what had been
a civil war between Vietnamese factions into a
war between the United States and Vietnam.

were clearly defined and the future predicted by the then president of SDS, Paul Potter:

> *The incredible war in Vietnam has provided the razor, the terrible sharp cutting edge that has finally severed the last vestige of illusion that morality and democracy are the guiding principles of American foreign policy. . . . This is a terrible and bitter insight for people who grew up as we did—and that revulsion at that insight, our refusal to accept it as inevitable or necessary, is one of the reasons that so many people have come here today.*
>
> *I wonder what it means for each of us to say we want to end the war in Vietnam. . . . There is no simple plan, no scheme or gimmick that can be proposed here. If the people of this country are to end the war in Vietnam and change the institutions that create it, then the people of this country must create a massive social movement . . . that we will build a movement that will find ways to support the increasing numbers of young men who are unwilling to and will not fight in Vietnam, a movement that will not tolerate the escalation or prolongation of the war, but will, if necessary, respond to the Administration's war effort with massive civil disobedience all over the country that will wrench the country into a confrontation with the issues of the war. . . .[2]*

As Paul Potter spoke, eighteen-year-old Thomas Bird prepared to go to war. Bird, like tens of thousands of America's youth, accepted the call to battle without hesitation or questioning. Many had grown up in families in which their fathers or uncles had honorably fought in Korea or the Second World War. It was not only their patriotic duty to serve their country; it was also a test of their manhood.

At eighteen, I went into the army to grow up and become a man. . . . I wasn't sure where Vietnam was but I was sure of our mission, fighting Communism. . . . It felt great. A noble mission in my life. I was going to do what my dad and other men of World War II had done. Save the world. We were 20,000 men and 500 helicopters and we were going to end the war in six months. Nothing prepared me for the experience soon to come.[3]

James Seddon of Iowa also felt himself to be upholding the tradition of American democracy when he arrived in Vietnam. He took his American history seriously, remembering how his parents' house was filled with the symbols of American liberty:

On the wall above the fireplace is a framed copy of the Declaration of Independence. Beside it is a bust of Thomas Jefferson. To me, that man and that document is the essence of America. The assertion that all people have a God-given right to life, liberty and the pursuit of happiness was my heritage and I was proud of it. The castoffs of their world had come together and raised the consciousness of humanity, believing that their country had a mission to enlighten the world, to eliminate pain and hunger. . . . That was what I believed America was about. That was what I was about.[4]

American soldiers arrived in Vietnam with both their ideals and their fears. Not knowing what to expect, they were astonished by the beauty of the country. Some who saw Vietnam for the first time from the air were struck by the variety of green foliage beneath them—dark green, light green, green with yellow. The landscape was exotic, and it seemed to some of the men almost as if they were on a vacation. One soldier called it "an island resort."

Because of President Johnson's escalation of
the war effort, in 1965 large numbers of
American troops began to land in Vietnam.

There were jungle-covered mountains and bare mountains. Trees danced in the wind—palm and banana, rubber trees, teak and bamboo. The young American soldiers were impressed by the whiteness of the beaches poised against the darkness of the surrounding jungle and the clear, warm waters of the ocean. Most were taken by the beauty of the people, the delicacy and grace of the women. James Seddon was so impressed by the Vietnamese that he saw his mission as something noble and sacred:

> *The people were like no others I have ever known but in some ways like all the people I have known. I tried to find things that made these people different from myself, but the harder I looked, the more similarities I found. The differences seemed unimportant. They drank weak tea, ate parts of animals I would have thrown away, looked and dressed differently and lived in strange homes, but they smiled when I smiled and we both hated what was happening in their land. They dreamed of the day when the rice would once again grow in their fields, children could return to school and the old people could enjoy the peace of old age. I dreamed of fulfilling their dreams.[5]*

Some of the soldiers who first arrived were personally welcomed by the commanding general, William Westmoreland, who came down to the beach to greet them as they disembarked from their ships—an event that was sure to make the evening news in America.

Once in Vietnam, the soldiers were instructed to write their mothers, telling them they arrived safe and sound. Their first packages from home usually contained cookies. Chocolate chip ones were the favorite. While some American soldiers were already involved in battle,

Many American soldiers tried to win the support
of the South Vietnamese by participating
in village life. Here an American GI teaches
Vietnamese children to play baseball.

in 1965 the war was still not a reality for most of them. Nineteen-year-old David Ross remembered the day he received a rude awakening. Clowning around in front of a military hospital with his buddies, they were interrupted by the roar of helicopter engines:

> All of a sudden, four choppers came in and they didn't set down. They just dumped bags. One of the bags broke open and what came out was the hardly recognizable form of a human being. All the guys stopped laughing. Nobody was saying anything. Some people were shaking, some were throwing up and one guy got down on his knees and started to pray.
> I said to myself: "Welcome to the war, boys."[6]

There was also the fear that every soldier felt whether or not he admitted it. William Maguire wrote this two weeks before he died:

> We're all scared. One can see this in the eyes of every individual. One might hide it with his mouth, while another might hide it with his actions, but there is no way around it. We're all scared.[7]

Raymond Griffiths had a premonition of his death three weeks before it happened:

> I'm going on an operation next month where there are nothing but VC and VC sympathizers. The area is also heavily mined. . . . All of us are scared because we know a lot of us won't make it. . . . It seems every day another young guy eighteen to nineteen years old like myself is killed in action.[8]

Most soldiers sent to Vietnam did not see action. Out of the 3 million Americans sent between 1965 and

1975, approximately 150,000 saw combat. For those who did, it was an experience they never forgot.

Jonathan Polansky was nineteen years old when he was called to war. When he returned home from his job one evening, his father told him, "Jon, you got a letter. I think it's from the president." Polansky had been drafted. He was all of 110 pounds, with a fierce desire to be where the action was. He got his wish. He was assigned to the 101st Airborne—a unit called the "Screaming Eagles."

Shortly after his arrival in Vietnam, Polansky, still a naïve teenager, was sent into combat:

> I had this big knapsack and all these things to put into it. I had no idea how to pack this monstrous thing. Older guys were telling me, "You'd better pack more water than that. . . . You'd better take extra grenades . . . to hell with the food, take ammo.". . . I must have been white as a sheet because I felt so scared. I thought I was immediately going to get killed.
>
> We had to climb up to the top of this hill. I had this pack on my back which weighed forty or fifty pounds. About fifty feet up the mountain, I realize I can't carry this monster. My breathing starts getting heavier and I'm struggling. I start to lose my footing because it's slippery and I start to fall. . . . I get so tired I get a pain in my chest. By the time I got to the top of the hill, I realized for sure I could not do this. I was willing to die right there. . . .
>
> I sat up that night. I didn't sleep and I didn't eat. I just sort of laid there crying and scared thinking about home. Just before dawn, . . . I'm sitting in the dew watching the dawn come up over the mountain when all of a sudden . . . I could hear pumf, pumf. . . . We were getting mortared. And nobody had dug in because we were all too tired. . . .

"Humping the boonies"—American soldiers
searching for Vietcong in terrain that made
it all but impossible to succeed.

I was wedged between a rock and a tree. I didn't even know where my weapon was. All I knew I was scared. . . . All of a sudden, crack, crack, we were being sniped at . . . forty or fifty guys start firing. Bullets and bangs and explosions going off all around me. I thought, "World War II . . . this is it, I'm in the war."[9]

7

WAR IN A SMALL VILLAGE

The arrival of the Americans changed the nature of the war for Le Ly and her village. Until then, the ARVN, the South Vietnamese Army, had established a moderate presence there, passing through the village by day, sweeping the area to search for Vietcong, and then withdrawing at night. They had not seriously sought to make contact with the enemy. And if a South Vietnamese soldier wandered too far or became isolated, he might be found with his throat cut or a bullet in his head.

With the arrival of the Americans, the war intensified in Le Ly's village. American and South Vietnamese soldiers were everywhere, intensely seeking to make contact with the enemy. They began to step up their artillery barrages and air strikes.

Finally, the Vietcong decided that the Americans and Vietnamese were vulnerable to an attack and they decided to strike. Le Ly and her friends were told to prepare for the battle by making extra food and bandages. The young girl saw weapons and extra troops being smuggled into the area by Vietcong, who hid guns in coffins and then staged fake funeral processions, the "mourners" being guerrilla fighters. Le Ly was startled to find that two of her former girlfriends who had left the

Increased terrorism by the Vietcong resulted
in South Vietnamese soldiers having to stand
guard while farmers harvested their rice crops.

village to join the Vietcong had returned—but with a difference. They were tough, seasoned soldiers, loaded down with weapons and snapping orders. They were not the same young women with whom Le Ly gossiped and giggled a year earlier.

It was Le Ly's father who gave the warning signal to the villagers when the Vietcong was about to attack. Despite the fact that there were soldiers in the village, he would poke the roof of his house with his broom as if he were clearing something out. The other villagers would then take to their homes. For some reason, the Vietcong attacked too soon. Mortar shells fell on soldiers and civilians alike, and Vietcong guerrillas popped out of hiding places and began firing at the enemy.

When the shooting started, Le Ly was delivering first aid kits to guerrillas hidden in a tunnel underneath a neighbor's bed. Le Ly was knocked down as three soldiers popped out of the tunnel and took up firing positions at the window. The noise was terrifying. The firing was wild and chaotic—anything that moved was mowed down with bullets from both sides. The house in which Le Ly was hiding was raked with machine-gun bullets, which tore through the walls, shattering pottery but miraculously missing everyone. Le Ly lay curled up on the floor, her hands over her ears, praying for the fighting to end.

Suddenly the Vietcong were gone. Cautiously, Le Ly peeked outside and, seeing that the village was quiet, made her way home. On the street, she saw a half dozen bodies sprawled near a burning truck. She recognized all but two of the bodies as local villagers. The others were Vietcong soldiers. One was still alive with shrapnel in his shoulder and a bullet wound in his chest. Le Ly went to his aid:

I put a compress on his shoulder as I had been taught to do in our midnight meetings, but the chest wound was sucking air, and although I timidly

*poured what little antiseptic I had over it, I knew
that the poor man would not live long enough to be
tended by a doctor. I tried to cover the bullet hole
with a bandage but the man twitched and yelled
and coughed blood so badly that I got scared and
backed away. I watched him squirm for a minute,
then . . . crawled back and said a little Buddhist
prayer in his ear and left him to his ancestors.*[1]

Meanwhile, the battle continued to rage in a nearby
rice paddy. It was now night, and the fields were illumi-
nated in an eerie blue light by popping flares while gun
muzzles "flashed like fireflies" in the trees. Helicopters
and planes began to arrive, dropping bombs and shooting rockets into the fields and tree lines. Le Ly found her
parents burying two Vietcong soldiers, rolling them in
mats and putting them in the earth. By morning, the
battle had ended. The Vietcong had withdrawn, claiming
that they had killed fifty of the enemy while losing only
eight.

After the Vietcong withdrew, the South Vietnamese
and American soldiers—whom Le Ly called "wild giants
who smelled bad"—entered the village in a rage. They
went from house to house, searching for Vietcong or any
signs that the owner had sheltered the enemy. They
burned the houses of suspects and took them off to
prison. Many were never seen again. When the Americans weren't terrorizing the village on the ground, they
terrorized it from the air. They bombed the rice paddies
and fields, pulverizing crops into dust, scorching trees into
fragments, and shattering rocks. The stiff dead corpses of
animals were everywhere—water buffalo with bloated
bodies "as big as a car," disemboweled pigs, and hundreds of dogs and wild animals torn by gunfire and shrapnel. Among the debris, the children discovered from time
to time the blackened figures of human beings, "charred
like wooden dolls from an oven."

The battle of Ky La brought a more dramatic change in the village's relationship with the Vietcong. The Vietcong became harsher and more terrifying. They began to hold special trials at night, accusing certain villagers of being spies and then taking them out and shooting them. The people of the village were caught between the Republicans and the Vietcong. As Le Ly described it:

> If the Republicans were like elephants trampling our village, the Viet Cong were like snakes that came at us in the night. At least you could see an elephant coming and get out of its way.[2]

The villagers were now under surveillance from both sides. Everybody began to mistrust everybody else. Strangers were regarded with suspicion. The Vietcong and the Republicans questioned the children constantly about every act and gesture of the villagers. Who talked with whom? Who visited whose house? How long did they stay? What did they say? The slightest suspicion could lead to a person's being killed by either side.

The situation became a nightmare for children. Once filled with patriotism and enthusiasm for liberating their country, the children began to lose their appetite for the liberation game.

> We were, after all, just kids. We could take only so many sleepless nights, endless hours in musty bunkers, unjust beatings at the hands of soldiers, and terror at the Viet Cong trials. . . . all we wanted was for things to return to the way they had been before the war started.[3]

But this was not to be. For one thing, the increased killing had orphaned many children. They wandered about begging for food, scavenging in garbage dumps, or stealing from farmers:

They wandered alone or with other orphans, look-
ing as miserable as they were. Sometimes they
played with other kids, only to stop when they re-
membered their situation and then move on like
ghosts. Most of the time they hung around like old
people, waiting for something good or bad to hap-
pen, for a little food or affection to come their way,
or for death—sudden or slow—to release them from
their suffering.[4]

The killings increased in frequency. Time after time, people would find bodies lying on a road or in a rice paddy. Who killed them or why was never known. Were they traitors, or was it an act of revenge? Did they work for the government, or for the Vietcong? No one dared ask questions, let alone answer them. To do so might mean being the next victim.

Le Ly was assigned the job of watching for Republican and American soldiers approaching the village. One morning at sunrise, as she began her shift, the fog was so thick she could not see her hand in front of her face. When the sun finally burned off the fog, Le Ly discovered she was surrounded by enemy troops, some of whom had already passed her station. She was in a dilemma. If she did nothing, the Vietcong would walk into a trap. If she attempted to run in any direction, she would be cut down.

Despite my terror, I forced myself to walk noncha-
lantly toward the road, right into the soldiers' teeth.
Every few paces, I bent to pick up a sweet potato or
low-lying berries that grew around the field . . . the
soldiers watching me from the corners of their eyes.
I hummed a little tune and paused even longer and
more often. "Surely," they must think, "there is no
more loyal Republican than this happy little farm
girl out gathering her family's breakfast."[5]

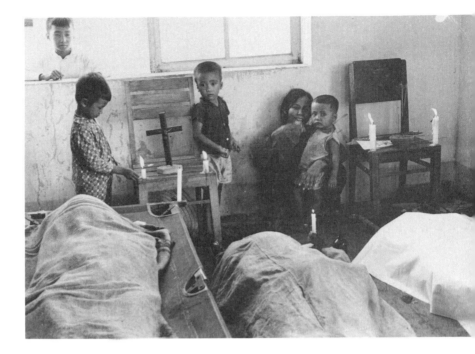

Vietnamese villagers maintain a vigil for
their dead. Almost 2 million Vietnamese
had died by the time the war ended.

Once past the soldiers, Le Ly was able to give the
signal warning the guerrillas that danger was near. Their
scout saw the message and ran to tell the others, saving
them from being massacred. Le Ly was considered a her-
oine. Several nights later, the Vietcong called the village to
a meeting and praised Le Ly in front of everyone. She was
called Sister Ly—after a famous Vietcong fighter—and a
song was written in her honor:

Sister Ly, who comes from Go Noi
Where the Thu Bon washes the trees,

Has defeated the horse-face enemy.
Her daily rice she could not eat
Without hearing the tortured prisoners.
Although the moon is covered with clouds
Her glory will shine forever.[6]

Le Ly's moment of glory was short-lived. Shortly afterwards, as she was hiding in a trench from intense bombardment, a group of Republican soldiers found her, accused her of being a Vietcong agent, and took her to a torture camp. She was taken to a room with a table that held electric wires attached to a generator, scissors, knives, razor blades, and a bucket of soapy water. Her hands were strapped to the table, and wires were attached to each of her thumbs. Her interrogator threw a switch:

> *A jolt of electricity knocked my legs out from under*
> *me and the entire room went white. A second later*
> *I was hanging from the strap, clambering [sic] to be*
> *let up. My lips were tingly and I could see my fingers*
> *twitching in the harness.*[7]

To prove he was serious, her torturer held up a short-bladed knife in front of her:

> *Go back to your cell and think what these things*
> *could do to your body. How would your husband*
> *or boyfriend or baby like you without nipples, or*
> *perhaps, I'll cut some skin off you for sandals and*
> *throw a few of your fingers to the dogs. Think about*
> *it Miss Viet Cong hero—then when you're called*
> *again, prepare to tell me everything you know.*[8]

Le Ly was taken back to her cell. But she refused to admit she knew anything. The next day she and several other girls were taken into the yard, tied to posts, and covered with honey. Le Ly saw that they were surrounded by anthills. The girls began to scream as the ants started to bite them. The more they squirmed and screamed, the more bites they received. Le Ly kept thinking to herself, "The ants want honey, not me," and tried to keep still. As a result, she was bitten far less than the other prisoners.

Despite the hours of torture under the hot sun, the girls did not break. Their guards brought out buckets of water, and one guard, reaching his hand into a bucket, took out a watersnake the length of his arm and dropped it down Le Ly's dress:

> *I knew from their appearance that the snakes weren't poisonous, but their bite was painful and the awful slithering—as they probed my waist, breast, armpits and neck, trying to find a way back to the water. . . . Whatever patience or self-control I could muster had long ago been exhausted. I screamed at the snake, screamed at the guards, then screamed at the sky until the noon turned black and my voice was reduced to a squeak.*[9]

Le Ly managed to hold on and not betray the Vietcong. She did not know how much more punishment she could take. Then, suddenly, without warning, she was released. Her mother had managed to pay a large bribe to free her. It turned out to be a major mistake.

The fact that Le Ly was freed so quickly led many Vietcong to believe that she was either working with the enemy or had betrayed them. Le Ly was ostracized. Then matters got even worse. While Le Ly was working in the fields one day, Republican soldiers were approaching her when they spied several Vietcong running in the woods. They killed one of them and captured another. Immediately, the village thought that Le Ly had set the Vietcong up.

The next night, two soldiers, Loi and Mau, came and took Le Ly to a meeting. It was a session of the dreaded people's court, and Le Ly was the star attraction. She was accused of aiding the enemy. The prosecution asked the gathered villagers: "What should be done with a woman who betrays the revolution? What should be done with a woman who spies for the enemy and betrays her comrades in the field?"[10]

The answer came back loud and clear: "Execute her, kill her. Teach her a lesson all traitors will learn from." One of the guards leaned over and whispered in Le Ly's ear: "There, do you hear that, Miss Ly? The sentence is death."

Le Ly was taken to a nearby swamp, which was unusual, since executions were usually carried out in front of a crowd. She was made to stand over an open grave by Loi and Mau, the two soldiers who had arrested her. As she waited to die, she was thrown to the ground, and Loi raped her.

> I now knew the horror that every woman dreads
> . . . the act of making life had left me feeling dead.
> The force of Loi's twisted soul had entered in me
> and killed me as surely as his knife. He could shoot
> me now—I wouldn't even feel the bullet.[11]

But Le Ly was not killed. Instead, she was raped by the other soldier and then allowed to go visit relatives elsewhere before returning to Ky La.

Yet the suffering was not over for Le Ly or her family. While Le Ly was away, her mother came home to find Republican soldiers in her house. They forced her to stand by the window and ordered her to signal to the Vietcong that it was safe to enter the village. Le Ly's mother stood by the window but gave no signal, hoping that no guerrillas would appear. Unfortunately, two did emerge out of the forest. As they approached Le Ly's house, her mother yelled out to warn them, but it was too late. The Republican soldiers rushed out to catch them, but the Vietcong fought back and were killed in the brief struggle. It turned out that the two were the men who had raped Le Ly.

Le Ly's mother and four other women who were supposed to be on watch were taken by the Vietcong and put on trial before the villagers. They were told that they should have warned the guerrillas even though it might have cost them their lives. The leader pronounced them guilty, made them kneel, and, putting a pistol to their heads, blew their brains out, one by one. As he was about to shoot Le Ly's mother, Le Ly's brother jumped up from the crowd and criticized the leader for shooting a woman who had so many members of her family fighting for their cause. The leader, aware that he had just killed four women without mercy, decided to make a show of leniency and spared Le Ly's mother. But life in the village could never be the same for Le Ly and her family. Shortly afterwards, Le Ly and her mother, telling no one where they were going, sneaked out of the village and headed for Saigon and what they hoped would be a new life.

8

THE WAR
AT HOME

In 1966, as the combat widened in Vietnam, the United States government added fuel to student fires already burning on college campuses. The Johnson administration decided to draft those students who were in the lower level of their class. Until now all had been exempt from military service as long as they were in college or graduate school. Now students would be ranked according to their grades. And a national draft examination would be given in order to determine a student's overall intelligence and achievements.

The antidraft movement spread throughout the United States. Students began to wear buttons that expressed their antiwar sentiment. "Make Love, Not War" was the most popular, followed by "Not With My Life You Don't." Others were simpler. "No!", "Peace Now!", and "Resist!" Students began to organize "We Won't Go" petitions condemning the immorality of the war and stating their refusal to go. One of the earliest read in part:

> Believing the United States participation in that war is a suppression of the Vietnamese struggle for national independence, we see no justification for our

involvement. We agree with Senator Wayne Morse that . . . "We should never have gone in. We should never have stayed in. We should get out."

Believing that we should not be asked to fight against the people of South Vietnam, we herewith state our refusal to go.[1]

Protests against the draft erupted on several campuses. Many were aimed directly at the university administrations which attempted to carry out the ranking system. The protests, which only a year earlier would have been carried out by a relatively few students, were now attracting increasingly larger numbers. One thing that brought about this change was the large increase in the number of students now attending college. In 1960 slightly fewer than 4 million young people were in schools of higher education. By 1966 the number was over 6 million, almost forty percent of those eligible for the draft. While only a few were radicals, they could mobilize support far greater than their numbers over the right issues.

Student protests escalated after it was discovered that many universities were deeply involved in supporting the U.S. government in Vietnam. The CIA and the military were funding a variety of projects, from civilian control to the design and testing of new weapons. Politically moderate student organizations also were found to be financed by the CIA. In addition, a number of universities were receiving federal and corporate funds for projects supporting politically repressive governments in South Africa and elsewhere.

One of the most visible signs of university complicity in the Vietnam War was the presence of recruitment centers for both the military and corporations supporting the war. Not only did students organize demonstrations against these organizations but they began to take direct action. In the fall of 1967, Dow Chemical Company—the manufacturer of napalm, a petroleum jelly used in bombs

Student antiwar protests escalated sharply
during the antidraft movement. Demonstrators
protesting the war outside the Pentagon
tried to convince soldiers to join them.

that incinerate their victims—opened up a recruitment booth on the campus of the University of Wisconsin. To students, napalm had become the most hated symbol of the horror of the war. Immediately, a group of students asked the chancellor of the university to ban Dow from recruiting on campus. The university refused, setting the stage for a showdown.

The protesting students then surrounded the Dow recruiting booth and refused to let anyone leave or enter. The chancellor called the police to disperse the students, which they did with great brutality. They began to club the unresisting protesters, breaking bones and causing bloodshed. Onlookers were so horrified and outraged by the police action that they interfered, freeing students who had been arrested and even attacking the police. The student body was so angry that, even though most of the students were not sympathetic to the protesters, they staged a two-day strike that brought the university to a standstill. The university finally compromised on the issue, and the chancellor resigned at the end of the year.

Campus protests against the war were one of the many forms of dissent that had developed. Student activists interrupted prominent prowar speakers and heckled them off the stage. Students publicly burned their draft cards, which was a violation of federal law, and some people were arrested, fined, and imprisoned. A popular slogan of the time was "Better to light one small draft card than curse the darkness." In all, some 200,000 people were accused of violating draft laws; 25,000 of them were indicted and about 4,000 sent to jail. Some individuals were sent to prison for as long as five years even though they had families and children.

As the war intensified, students began to take direct action, throwing objects at police such as make-believe blood to symbolize the blood being spilled in Vietnam. They resisted arrest and developed hit-and-run tactics to harass law enforcement officials and public figures who supported the war. Carl Davidson of SDS explained the new militancy:

> *No one goes limp anymore or meekly to jail. Police violence does not go unanswered. Sit-ins are no longer symbolic but strategic to protect people or hold positions rather than to allow oneself to be passively stepped over or carted off. Their purpose [is] the disruption and obstruction of certain events and actions by WHATEVER MEANS NECESSARY![2]*

In Berkeley, California, thousands of young people tried to block trains carrying military troops. The cry went out, "Stop the troop trains!", as thousands of students rushed onto the tracks and attempted to stop the oncoming locomotives with their bodies. Although the police tried to chase the students off the tracks by beating and arresting them, their efforts failed because they were heavily outnumbered. Despite the fact that students were sitting on the tracks, the trains refused to stop, and protesters escaped death only by jumping out of the way at the last second.

In addition to the change in tactics, there was also a tremendous change among young people. Until the mid-sixties, the radicals had generally been composed of the best and brightest of the student movement. They were organized into a number of groups collectively called the New Left to distinguish themselves from the Old Left, which was composed of socialists, communists, and Trotskyites from the past. SDS was the largest student group and one of the most effective on campuses. Its membership reached as high as 70,000 mostly white, middle-class students. There were several other groups from the Old Left whose roots were in the struggles of the 1930s. These included organizations such as the PLP (the Progressive Labor Party), Youth Against War and Fascism, Young Socialist Alliance, and Communist Party. In addition, there were broad-based antiwar groups such as the National Mobilization Committee to End The War. There were also a number of black militant groups whose focus was on black liberation rather than the war. The two most famous groups were the Black Panthers and SNCC, which had dropped the *nonviolent* from its name and became the Student National Coordinating Committee. SNCC, which no longer allowed whites to join, denounced the Vietnam War in 1965 as a colonial war between a powerful white nation and a poor non-white one.

Despite their reputations and the publicity surrounding them, these groups never represented a majority of students. Because students as a whole comprised only a minority of young Americans of their age group, the radicals were actually only a minority within a minority. However, they represented some of the most sensitive, idealistic, committed, and, at times, enraged young people of the generation. They demanded that America live up to its principles or, failing that, be overthrown.

Beyond the campus radicals, the mid-sixties also witnessed the rise of a new youth culture loosely referred to as hippies and sometimes "freaks"—a variation of the drug term *freaking out,* that is, "getting high." Many of the hippies were the baby boomers born immediately after World War II. Between 1964 and 1970 an estimated 20 million young people reached the age of eighteen. And while most led perfectly respectable lives, several million of them would at one time or another enter into the hippie counterculture.

The hippies were distinguished by their music, clothes, language, and attitudes toward sex and drugs. Their music heroes included Bob Dylan, the Grateful Dead, Rolling Stones, Jefferson Airplane, the Doors,

Jimi Hendrix, and Janis Joplin, entertainers whose song lyrics expressed a variety of experiences common to young people.

Hippies broke the bounds of conventional, middle-class morality by standing traditional values of respectability on their head. Many young people in the counterculture discarded conventional clothes and wore beads, American Indian headbands, colorful shirts and long dresses, jeans, bell-bottom trousers, cowboy boots, and sandals. Men wore their hair long, and sported ponytails, Pancho Villa mustaches, sideburns, and beards. Women stopped using makeup, let their hair grow long and unkempt, stopped shaving their body hair, and discarded their bras. Organic foods replaced processed ones. The emphasis was on simplicity and the primitive. One antiwar Vietnamese student leader remembered his initial impressions when he encountered these groups for the first time:

> Many of them were wearing raggedy clothes, often with the sleeves cut out of their shirts. Some had pieces of cloth tied around their wrists and bright rags bound to their pants or wrapped around their heads. It was if I had landed on another planet, full of creatures who found it impossible to take themselves seriously. . . . I concluded that these committed and enthusiastic antiwar people would eventually have a powerful effect on events in Vietnam.[3]

Sex and drugs played a large part in their lives. Drug taking was called "getting high," "getting stoned," or "freaking out." It was an experience almost all of them shared. The main drug most young people started out with was marijuana or hashish. Soon some began to graduate to more potent drugs such as amphetamines and even heroin. Hallucinogenics became a major part of the drug scene after Dr. Timothy Leary, a Harvard psychologist, experimented with a chemical called LSD, or "acid." Acid induced hallucinations—or visions, depending upon your point of view. These were called "trips" and the taker might have a good trip, in which the drug-induced experience was exhilarating, or a bad trip, which could be terrifying. A number of those who "dropped" acid never fully came out of their trips. Some remained in a psychotic state for a long time and suffered permanent psychic damage. But most of these people were willing to take the risks, and Dr. Leary set the mood of the era when he told this new generation, "Tune in, turn on, drop out." Tens of thousands did.

The result was that a youth culture developed that was different from any that had preceded it. Whereas previous generations of the young had sought to establish their own identity and emphasize their differences with older generations, the youth culture of the 1960s was a counterculture. It stood in opposition to the established society. Many who became part of it were high school dropouts, runaways, "teenyboppers," and groupies. Some were college students who felt burned out or disenchanted. The main enemy in their lives was their parents. Many of these young people had dropped out of society. Some limited themselves totally to drug experiences. Others went to live on communes, grew organic vegetables, or organized free food stores and free medical treatment to help fellow dropouts. They were opposed to the war and opposed to the society that America had become, but they were not inclined to do much about it. Some would participate in certain demonstrations such as love-ins and be-ins, which affirmed love and life; occasionally, they took part in antiwar demonstrations.

In fact, the radicals and the "freaks" were two sides of the same coin. Both groups rejected American society. The radicals wanted to change it; the freaks wanted to drop out. There were groups like the Diggers in California, Ken Kesey's Merry Pranksters, and the Youth International Party in New York—known as the Yippies—who launched outrageous assaults on American society. Jerry Rubin, a founder of the Yippies, distinguished a Yippie from a radical:

> *He didn't feel at home in SDS and he wasn't a flower-power hippy or an intellectual. A hybrid mixture of New Left and hippie. . . . A long-haired, bearded crazy mother . . . whose life is theater, every moment creating the new society as he destroys the old.*[4]

The Yippies would carry out shocking acts to call attention to the absurdity of American society. They used the media to their advantage to expose that absurdity. The Yippies publicly burned money or dropped dollar bills on the floor of the New York Stock Exchange, bringing all activity to a halt as brokers scrambled to pick them up. They planted soot bombs at the headquarters of Consolidated Edison, New York's electric power company. During a march on the Pentagon in Washington, Yippies confronted the heavily armed soldiers guarding the building by taking off their clothes, placing flowers down the barrels of their guns, and inviting the soldiers to join them.

The Yippies were court jesters and clowns with a serious purpose: to convince millions of young people—"the fourteen-year-old Kansas freaks who had let their hair grow long, dropped acid, and left home and school"—to break free from the tyrannical rule of their parents and have fun. They wanted to overthrow America, not by force and violence, as Marx and Lenin had advocated, but by sex and drugs. But there was a purpose behind this seeming madness and a utopian vision of the future:

> *Language does not radicalize people—what changes people is the emotional involvement of*

action. What breaks through apathy and compla-
cency are confrontations and actions. . . . The
struggle against the war is freeing American youth
from authority hang-ups and teaching us democ-
racy through action.

We want a communal world where the imag-
ination runs supreme and where human institutions
respond to human needs. Feeling and motion will
be unsuppressed. Everything will be free. . . . There
will be no nations, only rich communities and rich
cultures.[5]

As 1968 approached, the Yippies planned a major celebration to take place in Chicago in June, during the Democratic National Convention. Abbie Hoffman announced it as a "festival of life." He also denounced the oncoming Democratic convention as a "convention of death." "We demand the politics of ecstasy," he said. Instead, the underground radical paper called *Seed* warned:

Many people are into confrontation. The Man is
into confrontation. . . . Don't come to Chicago if
you expect a five-day Festival of Life, music and
love . . . Chicago may host a Festival of Blood.[6]

9

FROM RESISTANCE TO REVOLUTION

For three months, eleven hours a day, Troung Tang had walked down the Ho Chi Minh Trail leading from North Vietnam to the South. It was not a road in any traditional sense, just a small path in the woods. But over it had passed hundreds of thousands of men and an enormous amount of supplies and weapons to fight the war against America and South Vietnam.

Soon it would be January, the month of Tet, the new year, which was the most celebrated holiday in all of Vietnam. A truce was expected so that both sides could celebrate the new year without fear of attack. Yet, Troung was aware that something big was about to happen.

As he and his comrades marched down the trail, they passed tree trunks on which thousands of men who had gone before them had carved their names and their villages. To make the long march easier, the soldiers made walking sticks carved from a special bamboo called *song*. At night, they cooked food given them by villagers and dreamed of having a decent cigarette. Sometimes, they would catch fish by tossing a hand grenade in the river. Other times they would go without food for long periods of time. They wrote a good deal of poetry, for poetry writing was a Vietnamese tradition. Their poems would be about their loved ones, their country, and the day when there would be peace.

Like all North Vietnamese youth, Troung had been indoctrinated as a child by village teachers who told him of the crimes committed by Americans and the victories of North Vietnamese soldiers in the South. Ho Chi Minh was revered almost as a god. After each meeting, Troung would feel hatred for the Americans and a strong desire to serve his country. Yet, like many other young North Vietnamese men, when his time came for military duty, he tried to avoid the army for as long as he could. As one young Vietnamese soldier described it:

> While sacrifice was the theme, not all Vietnamese obeyed it. In my hamlet, I knew of at least eight other eighteen-year-old boys who delayed going into the army but the grown-ups all pretended they knew nothing. Some boys moved into other villages to live with relatives. You could say you were planning to get married next month or my mother was ill and I cannot leave her.[1]

Troung was aware that most of those who went south did not return. In fact, once a young man became a soldier, his family often gave him up for dead. But despite their fears, eventually most young men, like Troung, had to serve.

On the Ho Chi Minh Trail the soldiers were surrounded by danger. In the jungles they were often cold and wet and they caught malaria and other tropical diseases. They had to watch for antipersonnel mines dropped by U.S. planes. The size of a pack of cigarettes, the mines were wrapped in brown cloth the color of earth or leaves. When a soldier stepped on one, his foot would be injured and he would be more trouble to his unit than if he were a corpse.

The Vietnamese were terrified of the American B-52 bombers, which would drop giant bombs along the trail. A Vietcong veteran had once remarked:

> *You will never hear the approach of the B-52s. Suddenly there will be great undreamed noises around you, but you will never see the planes. If you're in the middle where the bomb lands, you will die. If you are close, you will be deaf for the rest of your life.*[2]

When, at the end of January, the North Vietnamese soldiers arrived in the South, the Tet holidays were about to start, but Troung was surprised to discover that instead of preparing for a celebration, the army was preparing for battle.

On the night of January 30, 1968, Herb Mock, an American soldier, was in a serious crap game at Dau Tieng when the attack came:

> *I was having this fantastic night in the track (armored personnel carrier), won sixty-five bucks and they were mortaring us. . . . It got really heavy. . . . They were firing on us from the woods. Helicopters started landing more ammunition. Jets were bombing in the woods. They'd hit and BAWWHAM! I mean the ground would shake.*[3]

The fighting at Dau Tieng was only a small part of what was happening all over South Vietnam. In every major city and at every major and many smaller military bases, the NVA (National Vietnamese Army) and the Vietcong launched suicide attacks. The fighting was fierce, and at times was reduced to hand-to-hand combat. The NVA captured certain cities and towns, but their victory was brief. Eventually, they were stopped and driven back. Tens of thousands of soldiers were killed.

The Tet offensive launched by the North
Vietnamese was a major defeat militarily.
Politically, however, it was a great success and
was instrumental in the eventual withdrawal
of United States troops from Vietnam.

Militarily, it was a major defeat for the North Vietnamese. But politically, it was a great victory.

For three years, the American public had been promised by its leaders that victory in Vietnam was near. The Vietnamese massive attack at Tet made them realize that the enemy was still strong and that the war would go on indefinitely. There were now almost 500,000 American soldiers in Vietnam—a 200 percent increase over 1965. Fifteen thousand had already been killed. Public opinion against the war began to change. Senator Eugene McCarthy, who had announced he would be a candidate against President Lyndon Johnson in the primary elections, stated:

> *In 1963, we were told we were winning the war. In 1964, we were told the corner was being turned. In 1965, we were told the enemy was being brought to its knees. In 1966, 1967 and now again in 1968, we hear the same hollow claims of victory. For the fact is that the enemy is bolder than ever while we must enlarge our own commitment.*[4]

The antiwar movement was beginning to find increasing support among middle America. Senator McCarthy's candidacy was followed by Senator Robert Kennedy's, who announced he too would challenge President Johnson. "I felt that I was being chased on all sides by a giant stampede," Johnson confessed to one of his biographers.[5] At the end of March 1968, Lyndon Johnson shocked the American people, and delighted the antiwar activists, by announcing that he would not be a candidate for reelection. He also announced that peace negotiations had started with the National Liberation Front. It was a major victory for the antiwar movement.

Several days after this, Martin Luther King, Jr., was assassinated. His murder gave rise to riots in Baltimore, Chicago, Washington, D.C., and Wilmington, Delaware. They were followed by a renewed outburst of student activity against both the war and racism. Students every-where were boycotting classes, holding sit-ins and teach-ins, and organizing rallies and demonstrations.

The high point came in April 1968, when Columbia University, in New York City, erupted. A small group of students protested the building, without community per-mission, of a gymnasium in a public park in the black area of the neighborhood by occupying the university presi-dent's office. Five days later, five buildings were occupied by 1,000 students. Mark Rudd, one of the student leaders of the action, expressed the sentiments of the radical stu-dents when he wrote the following letter to the president of Columbia, Grayson Kirk:

> *If we win, we will take control of your world, your corporation, your university and attempt to mold a world [in] which we and other people can live as human beings. We begin by fighting you and your support of the war in Vietnam and American impe-rialism. . . . We will have to destroy at times, even violently, in order to end your power and your sys-tem. . . . We, the young people whom you so rightly fear, say that the society is sick and you and your capitalism are the sickness. You call for order and respect for authority: we call for justice, freedom and socialism. , , , There is only one thing left to say. It may sound nihilistic to you since it is the opening shot in the war of liberation. I'll use the words of Leroi Jones, whom I'm sure you don't like a lot. "Up against the wall—this is a stickup."*[6]

After eight days of negotiations, no agreement had been reached. The students inside the building sang, de-bated, ate meals smuggled into them by sympathetic stu-dents on the outside, made love. There was even a marriage. At 2 A.M. on the eighth day, the police rushed the unresisting students and began clubbing them as they dragged them out. More than a thousand police entered the premises and arrested 692 people, most of them students.

A showdown was in the making, and it was to come in August of 1968 at the Democratic National Convention in Chicago. Two months earlier, Senator Robert Kennedy had been assassinated. There was anger and disillusionment among America's youth. A number of groups went to Chicago, each with its own agenda. The radicals wanted to protest the war and persuade the Democratic Party to support a peace plank. The Yippies hoped to hold a festival of life and reveal the absurdity of the convention. And there were a few who were seeking confrontations with the Chicago police force. The police were willing to accommodate them.

Most of the leaders of the protesters wanted to avoid a conflict with the police. They sought permission to march and demonstrate peacefully and to stay in the parks overnight. Even the U.S. Department of Justice tried to get Chicago to allow peaceful demonstrations. But the mayor of the city, Richard Daly, took a hard line. Every request was denied. Instead, 12,000 armed Chicago police and 6,000 National Guardsmen stood ready and willing to strike, even though the protesters were unarmed and, for the most part, were seeking only to peacefully express their opposition to the war. Peaceful or not, it made no difference. For five days, the Chicago police attacked and savagely beat protesters. They used clubs, fists, blackjacks, and brass knuckles. They punched and kicked women and children. They swept through gatherings of people chanting, "kill! kill!! kill!", clubbing demonstrators, bystanders, and journalists. Susan Stern, who marched with SDS in those days, found herself trapped:

> They [the police] closed in from all directions; from every street they came running with their clubs stretched out before them. . . ; and they came

106

smashing: heads . . . noses and teeth; flesh and blood. Blood streamed and splattered on me and I could hear the sickening thud of the club followed immediately by the crunch of breaking bones. I saw a burly pig swing with all his might across the face of a pretty young man and I saw the teeth spill out of his mouth, and I felt the sickness rolling in me. . . .[7]

Not only did the police attack those who came to demonstrate in Chicago, they attacked those who were working in the McCarthy campaign. They charged into hotels where delegates to the convention and campaign workers were staying and beat people in their rooms. For many young people who were there, as well as the many more who watched the proceedings on television, the police brutality in Chicago radicalized them. As far as the radicals were concerned, it pushed them even further to the left. Susan Stern remembered how she acted out her anger on the streets:

I began screaming chants with the crowd until I couldn't scream anymore. My arms were flying out in fists above my head and I pumped the air with them. I was boiling, singing, dancing, erupting with the spontaneous surge of freedom. . . . We gobbled up the night in a singing roar, violent and wild, saying we were on the side of the Vietnamese, on the side of freedom.[8]

To a small group of radicals, the police action and the politicians' refusal to adopt an antiwar plank proved to them that the only solution was a revolutionary one. Actually, an attitude change toward greater radicalism had already taken place several months earlier during an election of SDS officers. One of the candidates was a woman who was already a legendary figure in the movement. Her name was Bernadine Dohrn, and she had made the political transition from liberal to radical as the war continued and the civil rights movement began to stall. The assassination of Martin Luther King had affected her deeply. A friend remembered Dohrn crying at the news and then her tears turning to anger and rage.

> We went to Times Square and there was a demonstration going on. We started ripping signs and getting really out of hand and then some kids trashed a jewelry store. Bernadine really loved it. She was still crying but afterward we had a long talk about urban guerrilla warfare and what had to be done now by any means necessary.[9]

At the SDS convention, Dohrn was challenged about her politics by someone in the audience. Her response would set the tone for part of the antiwar movement for the next six years.

> "Do you consider yourself a socialist?"
> "I consider myself a revolutionary communist!"[10]

She was elected without opposition.

10

VIETNAM WINTER

America's soldiers had long abandoned their idealism. Beginning in 1969, the number who went AWOL—absent without leave—was four times higher than in previous years. Fragging (grenade assaults by soldiers against their own officers) was killing some 30 officers a year and injuring about 170 others. Drug abuse became more serious than battle wounds as the number of soldiers using marijuana and heroin began to increase sharply.

As 1970 approached, many of the soldiers had become demoralized by the sheer brutality of the war. Only occasionally did American soldiers directly do battle with the NVA (National Vietnamese Army), the regular Army of North Vietnam. Basically, the war was a guerrilla war with no clear front lines. Day in and day out, squads of American soldiers tramped through the jungles and the mountains—"humping the boonies," they called it—looking for the enemy. They swept the countryside on search-and-destroy missions, set up ambushes, and sought contact with the Vietcong, whom they called Victor Charlie, Charlie, or VC. The Vietcong would strike out of nowhere and then return into nowhere. They planted land mines and antipersonnel bombs that would explode

American soldiers engaged in a "fire fight" with the Vietcong. Because it was a guerrilla war, the Vietcong were able to surprise American forces by using land mines, booby traps, sniping, and ambushes.

without warning, killing men, blowing off their legs, sending shrapnel through their flesh. A man might see the head of his best friend blown off next to him or the soldier beside him lose his legs. When the Vietcong weren't using booby traps and land mines, they were sniping or raining down mortar shells or ambushing patrols in surprise assaults. Some soldiers witnessed twenty-four out of twenty-seven of their patrol killed in an ambush. Sometimes their best friends died in their arms or they had to pick up their pieces and stuff them into a body bag. Richard Cantale recalled the death of his best friend:

> His face was all cut up and blood all over it. His mouth was open. His eyes were both open. He was a mess. . . . After I left the place, I sat down and cried. I couldn't stop it. I don't think I ever cried so much in my life. I can still see his face now. I will never forget it.[1]

So brutal was guerrilla fighting that almost every soldier who saw combat and survived carried with him images of horror that he would never forget. Thomas Bird remembered:

> The fishnet full of dead Viet Cong soldiers from the hook of a giant helicopter that looked like a praying mantis.
>
> The rows and rows of dead Americans covered with ponchos.
>
> The grenading and collapsing of an underground field hospital that suffocated its screaming inhabitants to death.
>
> The disemboweled chopper crew hung upside down.[2]

Some soldiers, like George Robinson, were unable or unwilling to fully articulate their feelings:

I feel different now after seeing some horrible things and I'll never forget them. I can't say what I mean, but some of the things you see here can really change a man. . . .[3]

Another cause for disillusionment was the hypocrisy of the military and the U.S. government. This was a war in which many of the commanding officers gave rousing battle speeches while remaining in the rear in air-conditioned trailers while soldiers sweated it out in the jungle, where the brutality on the American side was equal to the brutality of the enemy, and where illegal military actions were carried out night and day despite political leaders' swearing they were not.

James Seddon, the Iowa soldier who had once believed in the righteousness of the war, had long discarded his beliefs after he saw combat. Assigned as an aircraft mechanic with five other men to dismantle crashed American aircraft all over Southeast Asia, his work took him deep into jungle terrain well behind enemy lines. Sometimes he would land in places where he was not officially supposed to be, such as Cambodia or Laos, places where the United States had a secret military presence that it kept hidden from the American people. He and his fellow soldiers became aware of the lies that the American government was telling the American people. They became increasingly cynical.

. . . the United States was breaking the rules. The government was telling the public one thing and doing another. It gave the impression that we were fighting this war with honor and dignity, like all other wars. The other guy does all the nasty stuff. I can't say for certain what this country did in other wars, but . . . I did know how they were fighting this war, and I felt betrayed. If what I was doing had honor

and was right, then why didn't the people who had sent me here acknowledge what was going on?[4]

There was also a great deal of confusion about exactly who the enemy was. Many American soldiers came to Vietnam expecting to like the people they were fighting for. They were attracted to the women and enchanted by the Vietnamese children. James Seddon recalled how he and a group of village children became friends:

The children were fascinated by the strange creatures among them. They touched our hair, rubbed our skin, and pulled our ears. When we reached out to touch one of them, they would jump back, laugh and return again once the hand had been withdrawn. They brought their bowls among us and we ate breakfast. When it was over, we were friends.[5]

Many soldiers gave the children presents, candy, and chewing gum, taught them how to play games, and helped them get an education. But the soldiers soon learned that the children could not always be trusted. Troung Mealy was one of those innocent-looking children of whom American soldiers became so fond:

I was ten years old when the Viet Minh convinced me to go to secret school. . . . At night they sat me in a cemetery, behind a grave mound. . . . In the underground school I read a book about courageous children. In one story, a courageous Vietnamese boy put his head into the barrel of a cannon to block it, so other soldiers could capture it. The child died. But his life is better than the ones who lived.

Sometimes they only train a child for one or two months before they send him somewhere with

a hand grenade. . . . Children were trained by the communists to throw grenades, not only for the terror factor, but so the government or American soldiers would have to shoot them. Then the Americans feel very ashamed. And they blame themselves and call their soldiers war criminals.

What happens to the psychology of any soldier—when a child throws a grenade and kills your friend, once, twice—you start suspecting all kids. It creates a very paranoid mentality for the visiting soldiers. They don't know which children are friendly. They start disliking and hating everybody. You believe you can't make friends with people in the villages because they are all trying to kill you.[6]

Many American soldiers, physically exhausted by the rigors of war, emotionally exhausted by fighting an enemy who was determined to win no matter what the cost, and filled with anger and rage at the deaths of their closest friends, often took out their frustrations on the Vietnamese people. Since it was impossible to physically distinguish friends from enemies, because many times Vietnamese who were friendly during the day were foe at night, tens of thousands of Vietnamese civilians were killed, many of them innocent. There were massacres of hundreds of women and children at places such as My Lai, and there were thousands of instances of killings of civilians in villages, fields, and rice paddies. Helicopter crews

Many American soldiers were enchanted by the Vietnamese children. They became personally involved with the children, giving them presents, playing games with them, and teaching them English.

American soldiers found it difficult to
adjust to the oppressive heat and humidity
in Vietnam. Here, it's cooling-off time.

indiscriminately fired at farmers working in fields, fighter pilots dropped bombs on them, and artillery shelled them, most of the time neither knowing nor caring if they were the enemy or not.

Another cause of the disillusionment for U.S. soldiers was the growing antiwar sentiment at home. They became aware of the unpopularity of the war among college students. It angered them that students could be deferred from serving and yet could protest against the war, while they, the soldiers, had to fight. One soldier wrote:

> I only wish I could do something to encourage the boys that are burning their draft cards to stand up and take their responsibilities for their country, family and friends. You can't defeat communism by turning your backs and burning your draft cards. Anyone who does it is a disgrace and plain yellow.[7]

Sometimes their anger was violently expressed. Greg Lusco expressed murderous rage towards the protesters in a letter to his editor:

> . . . how the hell do you think we in Vietnam feel when we read of the dissension and unrest in our country caused by the young, worthless radicals and the foremost runner of them all: the vile SDS. This is what we feel like: We have an acute hatred, an unfathomable lust to maim, yes, even kill . . . all of you back in the World.[8]

Gradually, many soldiers came to hate the war for what it was doing to them and their friends. They hated officers who demanded body counts, or who harassed them for petty things. They hated the jungle for its oppressive heat, insects and reptiles, and miserable weather. They hated the enemy and the Vietnamese people for whom they were fighting. Ultimately, the soldiers banded together, trusting only themselves. They wrote "Peace" and "Love," "Hate" and "Born to Kill," "Pray for War," and "Lover Boy" on their helmets. Like hippies, they wore love beads, headbands, and tinted sunglasses. They adopted thousands of Vietnamese dogs which they endowed with names such as Dink, Gook, Zip, Rat, Scag, or Trouble. Some soldiers even developed a grudging respect for their hated enemy while holding the South Vietnamese in contempt.

> The Viet Cong were capable of butchery . . . but they never sold their sisters, never licensed greed and there was no cowardice in them.[9]

In the end, they fought to stay alive and protect each other. "We fight for each other," one soldier said. "We're really tight here. Nobody else cares for us." Floyd Wilson, who was wounded and became a paraplegic (paralyzed below the waist), stated what the major purpose of every soldier was.

> The big trick was to stay alive. By that time all of us knew that Vietnam wasn't what it was supposed to be. We knew we were in a war like nobody else was in and our trick was to stay alive. And that's all. And staying alive meant doing what we did. God, if only some of this stuff would just have let your head rest sometime.[10]

There was no place for negative religious and racial attitudes on the battlefield, whatever feelings might exist in the rear lines. Stuart was the only black soldier in his company. While he was aware of racism among his fellow soldiers,

> . . . once we were in the field, . . . there was no color. I put my life on the line many a time for trying

118

to stop a white fool from doing something he was told not to do. Fortunately, I was never in a position where someone had to do that for me. But I'm quite sure they would have done the same for me. . . . I can remember being hurt at the death of my best friend. He was white. I cried like a baby.[11]

The soldiers also struggled to preserve their sanity, a struggle that some lost. James Seddon felt himself being divided in two:

In the past few months, I had begun to feel an invisible axe had split me down the middle. I had become two different persons and the person I didn't like was winning, while the person I wanted to be just stood by and watched helplessly. I was scared, scared of me. The world was becoming a different place and I was becoming a part of it. . . . The job of staying alive became an obsession. Every nerve ending had become raw from the intensity of the task. . . . I became a cog in the machine of war, a divided man, as divided as the country I was in.[12]

Albert Lee Reynolds found himself plunged into an abyss of darkness and despair:

I was struggling desperately to avoid being sucked into that whirlpool of death and destruction and sickness but it was no use. I went down—America went down—we all went down together.[13]

Perhaps all of these hardships could have been accepted had the American soldiers believed they were accomplishing something. The more the propaganda machine tried to convince them of the nobleness of their cause, the more they rejected it:

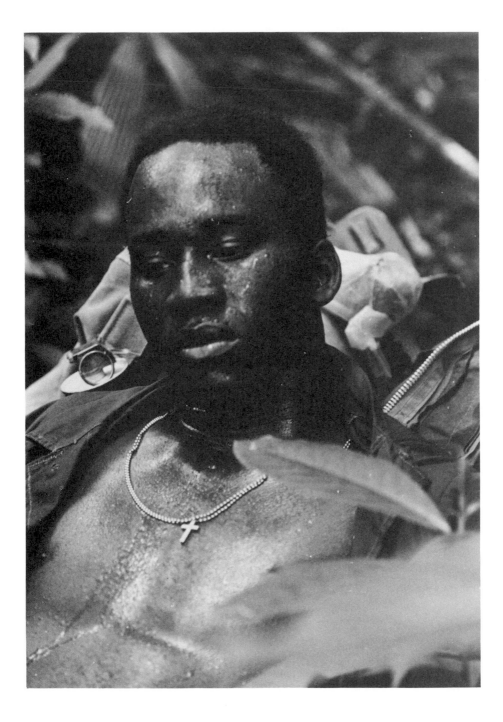

*We got the standard briefing, the one that was sup-
posed to convince us that we were on some kind of
holy mission. Knights crusading against the godless
hordes of Communism. God and history would
judge us heroes who went about the earth improving the lives of all humanity. I don't think any of us
believed what was being said. It was just standard
government policy, a page in a manual. Something
some jerk in Washington dreamed up to justify his
job. . . . We were more sure than ever that what we
were doing there would have no beneficial effect on
their way of life. . . . I grew to believe that there was
no solution to the problem of Southeast Asia.*[14]

Many soldiers recognized that the war had no purpose
and could never be won—that instead of saving Vietnam,
they were destroying it. Their job was just to kill as many
Vietnamese as they could without getting killed—and
then go home. Thomas Pellaton looked around him and
concluded:

*. . . the physical and human damage done over the
last few years is much greater than I realized—especially the human damage. There are the usual
scars of war all over—the bomb and artillery craters,
the ruined villages and the like. These things you
can understand as the by-product of war, but I can't
accept the fact of human damage. Not just the dead
but the GIs who can't talk in coherent sentences*

Although black soldiers were aware
of racism in their battalions, there was
no room for negative racial attitudes
on the battlefield. They were all in it
together, struggling to preserve their
sanity and stay alive.

anymore, or the ones who found out that they love to kill, or the Vietnamese, who must have once been a very gentle, peaceful people before the war turned them into thieves, black marketeers and prostitutes. . . . I feel like I'm at the bottom of a sewer.[15]

11
REVOLUTION AND REPRESSION

Between 1960 and 1965, the student movement in the United States had been marked primarily by protests against the war. From 1965 to 1968, protests turned to resistance. After 1969, for a small group of radicals, the time had come for revolution.

SDS, once an organization of nonviolent students, had split in two, with each group violently opposed to the other. Both had come to the conclusion that the only way to change America was to overthrow its present government and institutions and build a new society more receptive to the needs of its people. The two factions disagreed over the road to take to accomplish this goal.

One model for this militant attitude had been created several years earlier by the Black Panthers, a group of militant black men from the inner cities. The Panthers had publicly challenged white authority, carried guns openly (and legally), and been in shoot-outs with the police. As a result, they were attacked, arrested, jailed, and murdered. The Panthers' militancy won them much praise in the black community but little following. The only group that openly supported them was the SDS radicals, almost all of whom were white liberals. As far as they were concerned, the Panthers were the vanguard of the revolution. For their part, however, most Panthers regarded white radicals with contempt.

One faction of the SDS called itself the Weathermen, a name taken from a line in a song by Bob Dylan, "Subterranean Blues." The goal of the Weathermen was to "bring the war home": Their plan was to disrupt American life by carrying out actions designed to attack American institutions and rally support among those groups that they felt would be most sympathetic to violence and the challenge to authority—high school students and working-class teenagers.

> We've known that our job is to lead white kids to armed revolution. . . . We've been trying to show how it is impossible to overcome the frustration and impotence that comes from trying to reform this system. Kids know that the lines are drawn. Revolution is touching all our lives. Tens of thousands have learned that protests and marches don't do it. Revolutionary violence is the only way.[1]

Small groups of Weathermen began to spread out throughout the United States and live in communes. Their goal was to recruit followers among white high school students and workers. The Weathermen would hang out in pizza parlors, malls, anywhere young people gathered and talk to them about "liberating" schools, "killing police" ("offing the pigs"), revolutionary action, burning down schools—all tough talk to impress their audience. In some cities, Weathermen burst into high schools and held teachers captive while they lectured students about American fascism, racism, and imperialism. Their audience was usually astonished, puzzled, and sometimes hostile. One Weatherman noted this about the students:

*. . . they agreed that there were a lot of things wrong
. . . but . . . to get them to fight the police . . . to
attack the schools . . . it didn't make any sense. . . .
They wanted to stay out of trouble and make a
living. What you learn in SDS is that maybe you'll
get killed but the movement will grow and that's a
hell'va thing to go and tell a kid . . . he's gonna say
you're crazy.*[2]

After a while many of the teenagers became openly
antagonistic to SDS members and began to attack them,
chasing them out of neighborhoods. But they weren't
deterred. In fact, they saw rejection as part of their education as revolutionaries.

One major personal goal of the Weathermen was
"to get out of their white skin." They wanted to remake
themselves from the ground up. They rejected with contempt every traditional value and institution. Group members were constantly analyzing their actions and behavior
and mercilessly criticizing each other. The members of
the Weathermen were purging themselves in order to be
worthy of the revolutionary gods they had dedicated
themselves to.

On October 6, 1969, the Weathermen decided on a
public display of their strength. They announced that they
and their supporters would stage a major confrontation in
Chicago, which they called "Days of Rage." For months
before the event, they feverishly recruited high school
students throughout the country to join them. They announced that thousands, perhaps tens of thousands,
would flock to the city to participate. The leadership and
the hard-core membership of the Weathermen arrived as
planned and waited for the others to join them. The wait
was in vain.

Bernadine Dohrn rallied the disillusioned gathering
of 600 by calling them the "vanguard of the revolution."

Police haul a demonstrator toward a patrol wagon
as they break up an outbreak of violence in
Chicago in 1969. Armed with bricks and rocks,
the Weathermen, a radical faction of Students
for a Democratic Society, smashed windows
of stores and battled with police during a protest
demonstration they called "Days of Rage."

Their spirits revived, they swung into action. Dressed in motorcycle helmets and heavily padded clothes to absorb blows from the policemen's clubs, wearing thick gloves to pick up tear gas canisters and throw them back, and armed with rocks and bottles, they launched a major attack on the city considered to have one of the most brutal police forces in America. To the astonishment of several thousand officers, the Weathermen went on a rampage through the wealthiest section of the city, tossing bricks and rocks through store windows, smashing cars, even attacking the police themselves. For several hours the hit-and-run tactics of the Weathermen were successful. But eventually the police gained control and began to chase down, club, and even shoot the demonstrators. Six people were wounded, hundreds beaten and arrested. Yet, despite the police repression, the group was able to keep up the actions for several days.

Unable to attract mass followers by open rebellion, harassed by the police and federal government at every turn, the Weathermen decided to go underground. They broke into numerous small groups, went into hiding, and began to carry out revolutionary actions. A communiqué by Bernadine Dohrn from the underground announced their overall goals and reasons:

> We did not choose to live in a time of war. We chose only to become guerrillas and to prepare our people for war rather than become accomplices in the genocide of our sisters and brothers.[3]

Once underground, the Weathermen began a series of symbolic bombings of government buildings, including the Capitol in Washington, D.C., always carefully planting the bombs to avoid killing anyone. The Weathermen were not alone in this. More than forty radical groups at one time or another began to plant bombs. Jane Alpert was a member of one of these groups. To protest Nixon's bombing of Cambodia, she and her lover, Sam Melville, and four friends decided to plant a bomb in the Federal Building in New York City:

> *In the presence of us all, Sam assembled a bomb from a Westclox windup alarm clock and fifteen sticks of dynamite. . . . He placed the device in a large purse I had stolen from a department store. Carefully, I slid the strap over my right shoulder. The other five wished me luck. I felt very solemn, acutely conscious that I might never come back home. I saluted them and left. I boarded a bus headed downtown. I was wearing a white, A-line dress, kid gloves (to avoid leaving fingerprints) and a touch of makeup. I looked as if I were going on a business trip or to a matinee. . . . I was absolutely happy and, in spite of my raging pulse, I felt absolutely calm.*[4]

Alpert was able to make her way undetected to the electrical room on the fortieth floor of the building and plant the bomb. At 2 A.M., it exploded, blowing out the electric power but, like most bombings of the period, injuring no one. Tragically and ironically, this absence of fatalities was not to last. On March 6, 1970, a violent explosion ripped through a townhouse in Greenwich Village in New York City. Two women were seen fleeing from the wreckage, their clothes in tatters, both injured. Three bodies were discovered in the basement. Later it was revealed that the two women who escaped were Kathy Boudin and Cathy Wilkerson. The three who were killed were Terry Robbins, who was making the bomb, Ted Gold, and Diana Oughton. All five were part of the Weathermen underground collective. The bombing sounded the death knell of the group, and even though their activities continued for a while, their influence had ended.

128

The Weathermen's philosophy and militancy was shared by other groups, some of which were also dedicated to violence and also went underground. There was need for caution. Every law enforcement agency in the country, as well as the U.S. military, was looking to arrest them or members of almost any group that protested against the government. Vice President Spiro Agnew set the tone when he said:

> We cannot afford to be divided or deceived by the decadent thinking of a few young people. We can afford however to separate them from our society— with no more regret than we would feel over discarding rotten apples from a barrel.[5]

The message was heard loud and clear by law enforcement officials. Federal and state agencies used switchboard operators, college deans, students, custodians, and campus cops to inform on student activists. Police arrested people who had not broken any laws and framed others on drug charges using planted drugs. They harassed student leaders.

Nor did the law enforcement agencies stop at arresting protesters. They shot and killed unarmed students who were peacefully demonstrating or innocent bystanders at Berkeley, Jackson State, and Kent State. They killed Black Panther leaders under a number of pretexts. Prosecutors tried to send student antiwar leaders to prison for ten or more years. In many cases the appeals courts recognized these legal actions as intimidation and overturned them. But the court actions tied up people for years. Some were sent to jail while awaiting trial and spent thousands of dollars in court costs.

As the protests intensified in America, there was also a growing revolt against the war by many young people in Saigon. The impact of America on Vietnamese culture had been devastating. Doan Van Toai, a noncommunist student activist against the South Vietnamese government, recalled:

> *Then came the invasion of GIs. Tens of thousands at first, then hundreds of thousands. They urinated from the tops of their tanks and littered the streets with Coca Cola cans. Overnight there was an epidemic of bars. Prostitutes appeared in amazing numbers. The country was flooded with consumer goods that people hadn't even dreamed about before. Theft became a national industry—everything from sunglasses to refrigerators, from combat uniforms to the most sophisticated cameras. Everybody stole. . . . The Americans' material power was overwhelming, crushing, devoid of culture—except for a democratic idea; which was grotesquely caricatured by Saigon's rulers.[6]*

Tens of thousands of children were orphaned by the war, and many Vietnamese had lost relatives in the fighting or were refugees. The South Vietnamese were surrounded by corruption. They saw the rich bribing officials to exempt their children from the draft while the children of the poor were left to do the fighting.

The dissenters in Saigon were a mixture of Buddhists, Catholics, students, intellectuals, veterans, and people just tired of the war. Some protested because they were against the war and the corrupt society South Vietnam had become. Others sympathized with the Vietcong or were secret members of the Communist Party. But most were people who had begun to hate the war and all those who supported it—Americans as well as their own government. Student leader Doan Van Toai found himself in an ideological dilemma:

> *Caught between the NFL . . . on one hand and the Americans and their servitors, I and others like me*

As the Vietnamese watched antiwar protests escalate
in the United States, their own revolt against the war
began to grow. By the 1970s, protest movements
began to appear in South Vietnam.

supported the communists. At least they were Viet-
namese! Amid the quicksand ambiguities of the
war, here was a principle one could grasp hold of.
Careful, afraid, unwilling to commit myself, unsure
about what kind of a future I wanted, or about how
to get there, I knew a couple of things clearly. I too
was Vietnamese. . . .[7]

A fourteen-year-old girl in Saigon expressed the anti-American feeling that was growing among South Vietnamese young people in a poem entitled "Americans Are Not Beautiful":

They are called My
Which my brother says means beautiful.
But they are not beautiful.
They have too much hair on their arms like monkeys.
They are tall like trees without branches.
Their eyes are green like the eyes of boiled pigs. . . .
Their flying machines and their dragonflies
Drop death on people and animals.
And make trees bare of their leaves.
Here, Americans are not beautiful.
"But they are,
In their faraway country,"
My brother says.[8]

A group of South Vietnamese university and high school students began to attack American military vehicles and their drivers. They tossed plastic bags filled with high-octane gasoline into the vehicles and then ignited the gas with matches. One student explained:

I do not think the Americans understand the war in
Vietnam and many of them feel that their soldiers
are fighting only . . . communists. So if the Ameri-
can people see that it is the Vietnamese people in

the South who are hurting the American soldiers,
they will better understand the situation.[9]

At first, American soldiers fighting in Vietnam resented all the protests, both South Vietnamese and American. Ron Kovic, who later became a member of the Vietnam Veterans Against the War organization, expressed the reaction he and his fellow soldiers had when they first heard about the demonstrations going on back home:

> *I didn't want to believe it at first—people protesting*
> *against the war while we were putting our lives on*
> *the line. The men in our outfit used to talk about it*
> *a lot. How could they do this to us? . . . We swore*
> *they would pay, the hippies and the draft card burn-*
> *ers. They would pay if we ever ran into them.*[10]

But eventually, the protests made their way into the military. Throughout the war, a small minority of soldiers refused to serve in Vietnam. In 1967, Richard Perrin, a squad leader at the armored vehicles shop at Fort Leonard Wood, was having coffee in a PX cafeteria when he overheard two sergeants talking about Vietnam. One was describing how he tortured a captured North Vietnamese soldier by holding him against the hot engine of a tank. From that time on, Private Perrin began to investigate what was really happening in Vietnam.

In the summer of 1967, Perrin, to the astonishment of his family and friends, appeared at a press conference of antiwar GIs and handed out a statement which read in part:

> *I was being trained as a truck mechanic to work on*
> *armored trucks and self-propelled artillery. . . . I re-*
> *alized I was being trained to support these atrocities*
> *[in Vietnam]. At this point I decided to find out for*

myself whether there was any justification for the
war. Everybody said there was but they couldn't tell
me what it was. [11]

Arrested and sent to the stockade, Perrin was offered a compromise by the Army. If he agreed to stop the antiwar activities, he would be sent to Germany rather than Vietnam. Perrin agreed. But once in Germany, he witnessed what he considered vicious racism in the military. He decided to form an underground organization called RITA, which stood for "Resist Inside The Army." He deserted and eventually moved to Canada, where he joined civilian antiwar demonstrators who had escaped from the draft.

Perrin wasn't the only American soldier to refuse to serve in Vietnam. Hundreds of others refused to serve or joined demonstrations involved with the antiwar movement. Some were court-martialed or imprisoned for their dissent.

In Vietnam itself, as more and more American soldiers concluded the war was hopeless and even wrong, protest began to take many destructive forms. Some soldiers turned to drugs. Thirty-five percent of combat soldiers were estimated to be taking drugs, ranging from marijuana to heroin. Some combat soldiers killed or wounded officers who tried to make them take what the soldiers considered unnecessary risks. Thousands more signed petitions protesting or questioning the war.

Like Richard Perrin, John Young was an American soldier who made antiwar statements. What made Young's remarks unusual was that he was a prisoner of war at the time. Six weeks after he arrived in Vietnam, he was leading a patrol when suddenly gunfire broke out all around him. Caught in an ambush, Young kept firing back until he felt bayonets in his back. His leg was shattered.

Young expected to be killed or at least tortured.

Instead, his wounds were attended to and he received sufficient food to keep his strength up. One of the things that went through Young's mind at the time was what he would have done if Vietnamese had been prisoners of his. "I probably would have beat the hell out of them or shot them." It was during this time that Young began to think about the war. He remembered the bombings of Vietnamese villages by Americans, the forcible removal of civilians from their homes, the torture of suspected guerrillas, and the mutilations of Vietnamese dead by American soldiers. He started to read about the antiwar movement in America. Young began to change his ideas and attitudes about the war. In 1970 he sent a letter to then-president Richard Nixon condemning the war.

> *I no longer want to fight for you or anyone like you.*
> *I won't ever fight again for your American democracy.*
> *I will fight for my real American people and country.*[12]

He and other American war prisoners who shared his views were given better treatment in the camps. This angered other prisoners. Young was warned by an American officer who was also imprisoned in the camp not to communicate with the enemy. He and other protesters paid no attention. Two years later, when they were freed, the Army charged them with mutiny, including the charge that one soldier stated, "that the United States should not be in Vietnam, that the United States was committing atrocities against the Vietnamese people, that money to keep the war going was going to rich Americans and that American soldiers were killed for no reason. . . ." All charges were finally dropped, but not before one of the accused men had killed himself. In the North Vietnamese prison camp, he had once shouted, "I'll protest this war until the day I die."[13] He was true to his word.

By 1974, with the presidential elections on the horizon, President Nixon began to finally bring the war to an end. For four years he had gradually been withdrawing American troops from Vietnam while at the same time escalating the war by bombing North Vietnam and neighboring Laos and Cambodia, where North Vietnamese troops were taking refuge. These actions led to renewed demonstrations. In 1970, for example, over a million students throughout the United States went on strike at high schools and colleges to protest the secret bombing of Cambodia. Tragedy resulted. At Kent State University in Ohio, a conservative institution, the Ohio National Guard suddenly fired into a crowd of students who were protesting peacefully, killing four of them. A few weeks later, the Mississippi state police fired into a crowd of black students hanging out in front of a dormitory, killing two. Despite these outrages, the demonstrations continued.

In the final analysis, the determination of the North Vietnamese to win and the unrelenting protests in America against the war finally forced Nixon to make peace. By 1975, after a two-month period of relentless bombing of Hanoi, the war was ended. But the suffering the war caused for both the American and Vietnamese people continued on long after the fighting was over.

CONCLUSION

T he number of Americans killed in Vietnam between
  January 1, 1961, and April 13, 1974, was 56,555.
Almost 27,000 of those killed were twenty-one years old
or younger. Three thousand ninety-two were eighteen.
Twelve were seventeen. In the twelve-year period of the
war, some 2,340,000 American soldiers were sent to Vietnam and 115,000 of them saw combat. An estimated 1
million Vietnamese people died and 2 million were
wounded; 9 million were made refugees. Fifteen million
tons of bombs, 7 million from the air, were detonated on
Vietnam, four times the total used in all of World War II.

 With all this suffering and tragedy, what was accom-
plished? The Vietnamese communists were victorious,
but they are still suffering the consequences of almost
thirty years of unremitting warfare. The people of South
Vietnam are gradually resuming their way of life, but until
recently they had suffered much under the communist
government.

 American soldiers were shocked to discover upon
their return home that they were considered butchers and
barbarians. Frank McCarthy remembered unwittingly en-

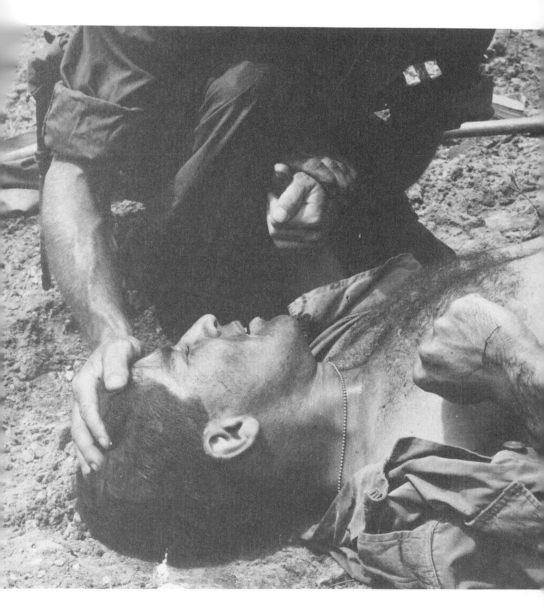

One of the many wounded American soldiers
in Vietnam receives aid on the battlefield.

tering a bar in an antiwar neighborhood in Philadelphia with his uniform on. Antiwar protesters called out: "You kill any women? You kill any kids?"

> *We went out to a dance that night. All I had was my Class A uniform. And boy it was such a shock. People looked at me like, "You scum." They'd walk by and spit on the ground. And I got this tremendous feeling that I had done something wrong. It was like I wasn't supposed to have survived.* [1]

James Seddon also was shocked by the reaction at home:

> *When I returned from Southeast Asia, the country was being torn apart by the war. . . . The streets were full of protesters. Everyone had an opinion about the war and students at Kent State died because of it. But no one really wanted to know about the war, the pain and the guilt. No one wanted to know what it was like to wash the blood of a friend from your hands. No one wanted to know about the guilt of leaving your friends behind and about not dying yourself. People were afraid to ask what was happening in Vietnam. They were afraid of what it might do to the foundation of their mansion. I lived in two worlds and could live in neither. I had nightmares about one and no dreams of the other.* [2]

For some soldiers, like Keith Franklin, the war was a waste of life. Shortly after he arrived in Vietnam, he wrote his family a letter which he instructed to be opened only in case of his death.

> *If you are reading this letter, you will never see me again. The reason being if you are reading this, I*

have died. The question is whether my death has been in vain. The answer is yes.

The war that has taken my life and many thousands before me is immoral, unlawful and an atrocity. . . . I have no choice as to my fate. It was pre-determined by the war-mongering hypocrites in Washington.[3]

Yet, there were soldiers who were willing to sacrifice their lives for a cause they believed in. Richard Marks, who was nineteen when killed, wrote this shortly before his death:

I don't like being over here, but I am doing a job that must be done—I am fighting an inevitable enemy that must be fought now or later.

I am fighting to protect and maintain what I believe in and what I want to live in—a democratic society. If I am killed while carrying out this mission, I want no one to cry or mourn for me. I want people to hold their heads high and be proud of the job I've done.[4]

Many soldiers were bitter that the United States did not go all out to win. They felt that had it unleashed its power against North Vietnam and against Vietnamese troops hiding in neighboring Laos and Cambodia, America would have won. Ironically, the United States won almost every major battle it fought against the Vietcong and North Vietnamese Army. Colonel Harry Summers

An American nurse works desperately in a makeshift hospital, trying to save the life of a soldier who's been wounded in battle.

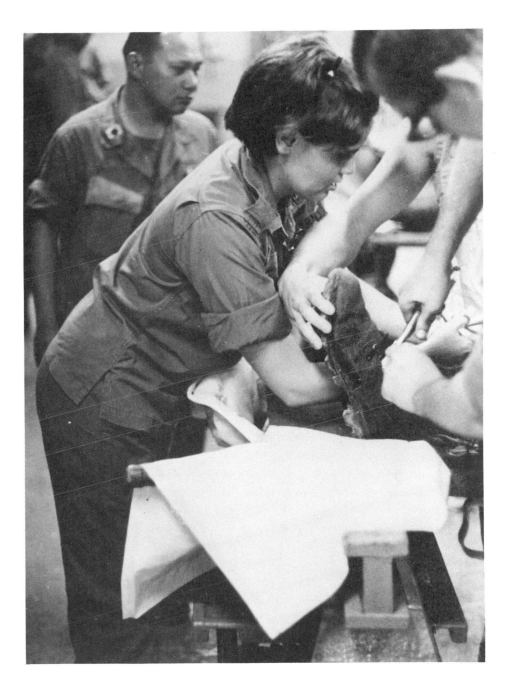

understood why so many Americans turned against the war and why the United States had not won a military victory:

> By 1968, the public had given us four years, their money and their sons. So I don't blame the American people. I do blame the national leadership, including the military leadership, for not setting clear and definable goals and objectives.[5]

For the protesters, the war had a variety of meanings. Pete Collier and David Horowitz, two antiwar activists who later switched sides to support the war, wrote in reflection:

> We hated the war but we loved it too. Vietnam made us special, a generation with a mission. The war justified every excess, every thought and deed. Heaving a rock through a corporation's window, we banished guilt by the thought: This is for the Vietnamese. Trying to set fire to a university library, we said to ourselves: This is for the Vietnamese. . . . If we committed small misdemeanors of indecency, they were in the long run justified by the much larger and more obscene crime in Southeast Asia. . . . Vietnam was in our marrow; it was our war, the experience that defined us . . . it was the time of our life, a fiery fountain of youth.[6]

A Navy sailor embraces his family on his return to the United States after his tour of duty in Vietnam. His ship, the Navy aircraft carrier USS *Coral Sea*, had been on war patrol for 331 days.

Tom Hayden, who went on to keep the faith and change the system by working within it as a state legislator, reviewed his life and remarked:

> The awakening of the sixties was a unique ingathering of young people . . . to try and carry out a redemptive vision. . . . The Gods of our parents had failed or become idols. Then a new spiritual force came in 1960 to move the world. We felt ourselves to be prophets of that force. . . . Then came rejection and both physical and spiritual martyrdom and later a discovery that we ourselves were not pure. We faltered, lost our way, became disoriented above all by death after death. We who claimed to be masters of our future, discovered we were not.[7]

For Le Ly, the escape from her village was not an end to her sufferings. For almost five years, she suffered abuses and indignities until she met an American in Vietnam who married her and brought her to live in America. Yet, long before that, Le Ly had found peace with herself. Having lived with death so many years, she finally learned how to live.

> I saw a determination to live, no matter what, was more powerful than a willingness to die. . . . Vietnam already had too many people who were ready to die for their beliefs. What it needed was men and women . . . who refused to accept death and death dealing as a solution to their problems.[8]

SOURCE NOTES

CHAPTER 1: PRELUDE TO A REBELLION

1. Tom Hayden, *Reunion: A Memoir* (New York: Random House, 1988), p. 14.
2. Ibid., p. 6.
3. James D. Seddon, *Morning Glories Among the Peas: A Vietnam Veteran's Story* (Ames: Iowa State University, 1990), p. 76.
4. Ibid., p. 26.
5. Ron Kovic, *Born on the Fourth of July* (New York: Pocket Books, 1976), pp. 60–61.
6. Jerry Rubin, *Do It!* (New York: Simon and Schuster, 1970), p. 18.
7. J. D. Salinger, *The Catcher in the Rye* (Boston: Little, Brown, 1951), p. 170.
8. Alan Ginsberg, *Howl* (San Francisco: City Lights, 1956), p. 9.
9. Jack Kerouac, *On the Road* (New York: Penguin Books, 1976), p. 11.
10. Hayden, op. cit. p. 19.
11. Hayden, p. 18.
12. Ibid., pp. 14–15.
13. Douglas Miller and Marion Novak, *The Fifties: The Way We Really Were* (Garden City, N.Y.: 1975), p. 281.

CHAPTER 2: PRELUDE TO A SECOND WAR

1. Stanley Karnow, *Vietnam: A History* (New York: Penguin Books, 1983), p. 107.
2. Al Santoli, *To Bear Any Burden* (New York: Ballantine Books, 1985), p. 135.
3. Karnow, p. 135.
4. Ibid., p. 147.
5. Ibid., p. 179.
6. Ibid., p. 178.
7. Ibid., p. 191.
8. Gloria Emerson, *Winners and Losers* (New York: Random House, 1972), p. 275.
9. Karnow, p. 195.
10. Ibid., p. 205.

CHAPTER 3: THE RADICALS EMERGE

1. Tom Hayden, *Reunion: A Memoir* (New York: Random House, 1988), p. 26.
2. Howard Zinn, *SNCC* (Boston: Beacon Press, 1964).
3. Ibid., p. 15.
4. Hayden, pp. 39–40.
5. Stanley Karnow, *Vietnam: A History* (New York: Penguin Books, 1983), p. 248.
6. Ibid., p. 250.
7. Al Santoli, *To Bear Any Burden* (New York: Ballantine Books, 1985), p. 83.
8. Hayden, p. 26.
9. Ibid., p. 93.
10. Kirkpatrick Sale, *SDS* (New York: Vintage Books, 1974), p. 89.
11. Ibid., p. 59.

CHAPTER 4: A *CHIEN SI* IS BORN

1. Le Ly Haslip, *When Heaven and Earth Changed Places* (New York: Plume, 1990), p. ix.
2. Ibid., p. 7.
3. Ibid., p. 18.

4. Ibid., p. 3.
5. Ibid., p. 35.
6. Ibid., p. 38.
7. Ibid., pp. 38–39.
8. Ibid., p. 40.
9. Ibid., p. 47.
10. Ibid., p. x.
11. Ibid., pp. 44–45.
12. Ibid., p. 45.
13. Ibid., p. 43.

CHAPTER 5: 1963

1. Al Santoli, *To Bear Any Burden* (New York: Ballantine Books, 1985), p. 98.
2. Neil Sheehan, *A Bright Shining Lie: John Paul Vann, An American in Vietnam* (New York: Random House, 1988), p. 291.
3. Santoli, *To Bear Any Burden,* p. 114.
4. Al Santoli, *Everything We Had* (New York: Ballantine Books, 1981), p. 10.
5. Ibid., p. 11.
6. Tom Hayden, *Reunion: A Memoir* (New York: Random House, 1988), p. 114.

CHAPTER 6: RESISTANCE AND WAR

1. Stanley Karnow, *Vietnam: A History* (New York: Penguin Books, 1983), p. 412.
2. Kirkpatrick Sale, *SDS* (New York: Vintage Books, 1974), pp. 111–114.
3. *New York Times,* May 27, 1990.
4. James D. Seddon, *Morning Glories Among the Peas: A Vietnam Veteran's Story* (Ames: Iowa State University, 1990), p. 105.
5. Ibid., p. 42.
6. Al Santoli, *Everything We Had* (New York: Ballantine Books, 1981), p. 3.

7. Bernard Edelman, *Dear America: Letters Home From Vietnam* (New York: Pocket Books, 1985), p. 118.
8. Al Santoli, *Everything We Had,* p. 50.
9. Al Santoli, *To Bear Any Burden,* p. 103.

CHAPTER 7: WAR IN A SMALL VILLAGE

1. Le Ly Haslip, *When Heaven and Earth Changed Places* (New York: Plume, 1990), pp. 67–68.
2. Ibid., p. 69.
3. Ibid., p. 70.
4. Ibid., p. 69.
5. Ibid., p. 72.
6. Ibid., p. 75.
7. Ibid., p. 82.
8. Ibid.
9. Ibid., p. 84.
10. Ibid., p. 89.
11. Ibid., p. 93.

CHAPTER 8: THE WAR AT HOME

1. Alice Lynd, *We Won't Go* (Boston: Beacon Press, 1968), p. 203.
2. Kirkpatrick Sale, *SDS* (New York: Vintage Books, 1974), p. 381.
3. Doan Van Roai, *The Vietnamese Gulag* (New York: Simon and Schuster, 1986), p. 324.
4. Jerry Rubin, *Do It!* (New York: Simon and Schuster, 1970), p. 82.
5. Ibid., pp. 250–251.
6. Todd Gitlin, *The Sixties: Years of Hope, Days of Rage* (New York: Bantam, 1987), p. 324.

CHAPTER 9: FROM RESISTANCE TO REVOLUTION

1. Gloria Emerson, *Winners and Losers* (New York: Random House, 1972), pp. 75–76.

2. Ibid., p. 76.
3. Al Santoli, *Everything We Had* (New York: Ballantine Books, 1981), p. 83.
4. Todd Gitlin, *The Sixties: Years of Hope, Days of Rage* (New York: Bantam, 1987), p. 299.
5. Ibid., p. 302.
6. "Communism and the New Left," *U.S. News and World Report,* 1969, pp. 115–116.
7. Susan Stern, *With the Weathermen* (Garden City, N.Y.: Doubleday, 1975), p. 24.
8. Ibid.
9. Kirkpatrick Sale, *SDS* (New York: Vintage Books, 1974), p. 425.
10. Ibid., p. 451.

CHAPTER 10: VIETNAM WINTER
1. Bernard Edelman, *Dear America: Letters Home From Vietnam* (New York: Pocket Books, 1985), p. 207.
2. *New York Times,* May 27, 1990.
3. Edelman, pp. 87–88.
4. James D. Seddon, *Morning Glories Among the Peas: A Vietnam Veteran's Story* (Ames: Iowa State University, 1990), p. 35.
5. Ibid., p. 61.
6. Al Santoli, *To Bear Any Burden* (New York: Ballantine Books, 1985), pp. 58–61.
7. Gloria Emerson, *Winners and Losers* (New York: Random House, 1972), p. 99.
8. Edelman, pp. 239–240.
9. Gloria Emerson, p. 62.
10. Personal interview with author, 1989.
11. Santoli, *To Bear Any Burden,* p. 135.
12. Seddon, p. 35.
13. Emerson, p. 27.
14. Seddon, p. 42.
15. Edelman, p. 90.

CHAPTER 11: REVOLUTION AND REPRESSION

1. Kirkpatrick Sale, *SDS* (New York: Vintage Books, 1974), p. 631.
2. Ibid., pp. 582–583.
3. Ibid., p. 572.
4. Susan Stern, *With the Weathermen* (Garden City, N.Y.: Doubleday, 1975), pp. 212–213.
5. Sale, p. 642.
6. Gloria Emerson, *Winners and Losers* (New York: Random House, 1972), p. 106.
7. Doan Van Toai and David Chanoff, *The Vietnam Gulag* (New York: Simon and Schuster, 1986), p. 142.
8. Emerson, p. 242.
9. Ibid., p. 105.
10. Ron Kovic, *Born on the Fourth of July* (New York: Pocket Books, 1976), p. 134.
11. Emerson, p. 167.
12. Ibid., p. 232.
13. Ibid., p. 233.

CONCLUSION

1. Al Santoli, *To Bear Any Burden* (New York: Ballantine Books, 1985), p. 109.
2. James D. Seddon, *Morning Glories Among the Peas: A Vietnam Veteran's Story* (Ames: Iowa State University, 1990), p. 128.
3. Gloria Emerson, *Winners and Losers* (New York: Random House, 1972), p. 101.
4. Bernard Edelman, *Dear America: Letters Home From Vietnam* (New York: Pocket Books, 1985), p. 113.
5. Santoli, *To Bear Any Burden,* p. 175.
6. Peter Collier and David Horowitz, *Destructive Generation* (New York: Summit Books, 1989), pp. 290–291.
7. Tom Hayden, *Reunion: A Memoir* (New York: Random House, 1988), p. 505.
8. Le Ly Haslip, *When Heaven and Earth Changed Places* (New York: Plume, 1990), p. 215.

FOR FURTHER READING

THE PROTEST

Alpert, Jane. *Growing Up Underground.* New York: Citadel Underground Press, 1990.

Cluster, Dick, ed. *They Should Have Served That Cup of Coffee: 7 Radicals Remember the 60s.* Boston: South End Press, 1979.

Collier, Peter, and Horowitz, David. *Destructive Generation.* New York: Summit Books, 1989.

"Communism and the New Left." *U.S. News and World Report,* 1969.

Gitlin, Todd. *The Sixties, Years of Hope, Days of Rage.* New York: Bantam Books, 1987.

Halstead, Fred. *Out Now!* New York: Monad Press, 1978.

Hayden, Tom. *Reunion: A Memoir.* New York: Random House, 1988.

Lynd, Alice. *We Won't Go.* Boston: Beacon Press, 1968.

Morrison, Joan, and Morrison, Robert K. *From Camelot to Kent State.* New York: Times Books, 1987.

Payne, Cril. *Deep Cover.* New York: Newsweek Books, 1979.

Rubin, Jerry. *Do It!* New York: Simon and Schuster, 1970.

Sale, Kirkpatrick. *SDS.* New York: Vintage Books, 1974.

Stern, Susan. *With the Weathermen.* Garden City, N.Y.: Doubleday, 1975.

Zinn, Howard. *SNCC.* Boston: Beacon Press, 1964.

THE WAR

Edelman, Bernard. *Dear America: Letters From Vietnam.* New York: Pocket Books, 1985.

Emerson, Gloria. *Winners and Losers.* New York: Random House, 1972.

Karnow, Stanley. *Vietnam: A History.* New York: Penguin Books, 1983.

Kovic, Ron. *Born on the Fourth of July.* New York: Pocket Books, 1976.

Santoli, Al. *Everything We Had.* New York: Ballantine Books, 1981.

Santoli, Al. *To Bear Any Burden.* New York: Ballantine Books, 1985.

Seddon, James D. *Morning Glories Among the Peas: A Vietnam Veteran's Story.* Ames: Iowa State University, 1990.

Sheehan, Neil. *A Bright Shining Lie: John Paul Vann, an American in Vietnam.* New York: Random House, 1985.

THE VIETNAMESE

Doyon, Jacques. *Les Viet Cong.* Paris: Editions de Noel, 1968.

Haslip, Le Ly. *When Heaven and Earth Changed Places.* New York: Plume, 1989.

Van Toai, Doan, and Chanoff, David. *The Vietnamese Gulag.* New York: Simon and Schuster, 1986.

INDEX

Page numbers in *italics* refer to illustrations.

ABOUT THE AUTHOR

Richard L. Wormser has written and/or provided the photography for numerous juvenile and young adult books. He has also written, produced, and directed over one hundred films, videotapes, and slide presentations for television, industry, educational institutions, and government organizations. Mr. Wormser was active in the civil rights and antiwar movements, but was opposed to criticism of the enlisted soldiers who bore so much of the suffering.

GEORGE ROGERS CLARK
LIBRARY MEDIA CENTER